In today's digital and distracted world, 24 Hours are ~~not~~ enough

HOW TO MANUFACTURE TIME?

In today's digital and distracted world, 24 Hours are ~~not~~ enough

HOW TO MANUFACTURE TIME?

CHANDAN GOYAL

Gullybaba Publishing House Pvt. Ltd

GULLYBABA PUBLISHING HOUSE PVT. LTD.
ISO 9001 & ISO 14001 CERTIFIED CO.
Regd. Office: 2525/193, 1st Floor, Onkar Nagar-A, Tri Nagar, Delhi-110035, (From Kanhaiya Nagar Metro Station Towards Old Bus Stand)
Branch Office: 1A/2A, 20, Hari Sadan, Ansari Road, Daryaganj, New Delhi-110002
Ph.: 09350849407, 011-27387998
E-mail: info@gullybaba.com
Websites: GullyBaba.com

First Edition: 2020
Price: ₹399/-
ISBN: 978-93-89601-31-2

Layout Design: Gullybaba Publishing House Pvt. Ltd.

CONTENTS

PRAISE

for the book

"Like in every other areas of life, implementation is the key. However, the way Chandan has shared the tools and habits, it was a child's play to implement and get the instant results. It can't be simpler than this, it's a must read Classic on Time."

Sachin Kharbanda
Managing Director
Lakshita Fashions Pvt. Ltd.

"The simplicity and practicality of tools engrossed me so much that I couldn't put down this book once I started reading."

Deepak Methi
President
Pankaj Electronics

"Feel like I am having 36 hours in a day. My whole orientation about time got shifted. I was shocked to confront that I was operating from the schedules of people around me. Now, I feel very light and empowered."

Kamal Tyagi
Founder & CEO
Pinga One ERP

"I can't thank Chandan much for such a simplified but highly effective ISD Framework for creating time. It's working like a Genie for me. I wish I would have access to this technology 10 years back."

Rajiv Gandhi
Principal Architect & CEO
Design Forum of Architects (DSA)

"Transformative read. This book is going to be New York Times Bestseller."

Dinesh Verma
Author & Publisher

"DDS is actually the Brahmashtra of all the tools in this book. It's like being in a state of Flow. In today's distracted world, DDS is my competitive edge which I was looking for. Bonus habits are like cherries on the cake."

Mitul Jain
Managing Director
Mitzvah Air Curtains

"I was quite apprehensive whether it's just another time management book. I was proven wrong before I had completed 1/4th of the book and my myths about time management were blown away. I am creating time like magic and people around me are simply wondering what I have done to myself."

Amit Singhal
Director
Facets Clothing Co.

WHY THIS BOOK?

I came to Delhi in 1995 to pursue graduation from Delhi University. Kirori Mal College was very close to Kamla Nagar market in North Delhi and I was in hostel. I remember that going to Kamla Nagar market with friends in the evening time was a sort of ritual. We used to spend 60-90 minutes over there in the company of some tea and snacks. That time, there were no mobile phones and almost everything was manual. I remember that to withdraw money from my bank account in Corporation Bank, it took minimum 30 minutes and that too when Corporation bank was one of the most efficient banks that time. We used to reach picture halls almost one hour before the movie time so that we could buy the tickets at actual price instead of buying in black at higher price later on. In spite of no automation or technology, I used to have good amount of spare time along with my studies. Not to brag, but just to inform that I used to spend good amount of time on studies, I came third in Delhi University in my graduation.

Fast forward 2015, I am an entrepreneur, co-founder of a company with more than 100 employees. Every utility around me is online i.e. movie ticket, banking, flight and—train tickets, hotel booking, electricity bill, cab, books, food- you just name it and it's there. The most common and irritating phrase I get to hear from people is "I don't have time." I always wonder: why is it so!! I have more time in my life despite of the fact that I am married and heading a company. However, the real catch was the reason of people getting no time and me getting more time was same- guess what- *technology.*

The only difference was that I was using the technology and in case of people who complained about lack of time, technology was using them. When I shared my habits and how I use the technology to create more time, people were simply awestruck. These simple insights added hundreds of hours in their life, which made them happier and healthier. They started living their life from 'this *or* that' to 'this *and* that'.

Then I started getting requests for the workshops in corporates on how to create more time. People requested me to write a book on how they can have more time in their life. I experimented with a series of blogs on LinkedIn on this topic and it was well appreciated by people. I felt so happy that I could make a significant difference in people's life.

To spread this know-how of creating time at mass level, book is the best choice. This book is a live testimony that even a book can be written using the tools and techniques, which I have shared here.

It pains me when I look at the time poverty, which people have created in their life. My mission is to add at least 1,000 hours per year to people's life, which they are wasting without knowing.

ACKNOWLEDGEMENTS

Life is a learning school. We all keep learning till our last breath. People whom we come across during the journey of life usually inspire us.

This is my first book and I feel grateful to lots of people in my life to make this happen. I take this opportunity to express my gratitude for the learning, inspiration and support which made it possible for me to write this book.

My mother and Grandfather have been the biggest influencers in creating and living the time creation habits. It is said that majority of our brain and learning happens in the initial 5-10 years of our life. In my case too, when I look back, I imbibed some of the amazing habits of my grandfather and the biggest of them is getting up early. This simple habit helped me a lot in my academic career and maintaining a good health as well.

My mother groomed me to be an organized person since early childhood, though unconsciously. We were four siblings and we were staying with our grandparents. There used to be a regular influx of relatives as we had a very big joint family. In spite of taking care of all household activities single handedly (as my grandmother was very old), she was very mindful of grooming each one of us, but I got the largest share of her grooming being the first child.

The biggest influence in my corporate career (albeit a short one) was of Rajeev Grover and Sanjeev Verma whom we fondly referred as RG and SV. RG is the managing director of HLS Asia Limited (it's a joint venture between Halliburton Logging Inc. and Austin Energy Pvt. Ltd.). RG used to reach office half an hour early but left office on time. I have never seen RG sitting late on any day till the time I worked there. He is a very simple man, but his habits of organising himself were amazing. I feel immensely grateful to RG for organising a corporate session with his dear friend Bharat Bhushan Kapur. Till date, I am practising one habit (related to e-mail management) shared by Bharat in 2003.

SV was heading the Operations at HLS Asia Limited, which was the most time consuming and client facing activity. Still, SV managed his day in such a way that he reached office by 8.30am and left sharply by 5.45pm. No paper dared to sit on his table beyond the day. I deeply admire his instant decision making skill, which I am still learning.

After I started my entrepreneurial journey in 2005 by co-founding Blue Consulting Private Limited, I got the opportunity to interact with lots of senior people at CXO level, which made me learn a lot about time guarding and time creation. One such person who stands out is my dear friend and coach Rahul Jain. Rahul is the pioneer and one of the most successful Business Coaches in India. His simple yet highly effective time creating habits helped me to achieve amazing results in my business and personal life.

Now comes the person who influenced me the most

to write this book. He is my dear friend, mentor and the maverick marketing guru Akshar Yadav. A chance meeting with Akshar at a café sowed the seed for this book.

Here is a special acknowledgement to the most special person in my life- my friend, my girlfriend and of course my wife- Dolly who plays these three roles in my life. She was the happiest when I shared with her that I am writing a book and she checked with me many times before it got published. Her belief and enthusiasm motivated me to complete it even though there were some moments of doubt when I thought of leaving it midway.

Finally, this book could not have been possible without the ultimate support of my friend and publisher Dinesh Verma who put in personal effort to follow up, designing and publishing this book on time.

INTRODUCTION

Picking up this book clearly indicates that you are a learner and want to manufacture time for the things, which matters to you, for which you have no time in life. Not to disappoint, but let me clarify in the beginning itself that this books is not about time management, rather it would be just one side benefit out of major other benefits which you are going to reap.

This book is about the fundamental truth of your relationship with time. Let's do a small exercise. Just close your eyes and remember the period 10 years back or 20 years back. Go through your daily routine, inspect the state of your body, the strength of your relationship, outdoor activities and your entertainment sources. Now, open your eyes, and take stock of your present state of affairs.

Do you think that nature has reduced the time nowadays? No, that's not the case. Then why we feel that we don't have time these days? When you ask this question, you may get following types of answers:

1. People are after the material wealth.
2. People have become very selfish and self-centred.
3. Nuclear family system has caused this.

4. We are influenced by the Western culture.
5. Social media is the main culprit.

If you observe life closely, time is the only democratic allotment of resources to all humans on this planet. Everybody has the same amount of time, which is 24 hours or 1,440 minutes or 86,400 seconds in one day. A super successful also has the same 24 hours in a day when we compare it with the time available with a day laborer.

When you analyse the situation 10 or 20 years back and relate to that time with a happy state of mind, it's mainly because you think that during that time you had almost no pressure to perform in any areas of your life.

However, if you really compare that time with the present time on apple to apple basis, you would be surprised to know that the present time is much more better than the previous one. I am sure, the moment you read this last line, a big "No' or "I disagree" crossed your mind.

Let me help you to understand this. Would you agree that in earlier days there were very limited choices or rather no choices in many areas of our life i.e. communication (read phone), entertainment, transportation, accommodation, electricity, health, medical facilities?

Today, you have plenty of choices in each of these areas that we just discussed.

Earlier, because of limitation of choices, a person was required to spend very less energy and thinking about choosing a particular model or type of thing. Further, even if many choices were available earlier, but availability of information about them to compare was either not there or it was very limited.

If you compare the quality and convenience of material things of previous time with that of today's, the later will score much higher. In spite of so much comfort, convenience, choices and information, why we feel chocked or pressurised all the time?

Reason is quite a simple one—with more choices, choices for distraction have also increased.

Initially, when use of technology took off in the form of Internet and mobile phone, we were using the technology for our convenience and comfort. However, today it's completely opposite, this very same technology-mobile and Internet is using us. Instead of mastering technology or being master of technology, we have become the slave of technology. I would like to clarify that when I am saying that we have become slave of technology, I am no way saying that we should not use technology and switch back to our old days of doing things.

I consider myself very fortunate to develop an awareness that technology is a means to an end and not an end itself. Just because of this awareness, I could take following extreme steps with ease and comfort:

1. Not having TV at home since the time I came to Delhi in 1995.
2. I don't read national newspaper since 2008.
3. Removal of e-mail App from my phone.
4. Non-syncing of all my devices (read Phone, Tab and Laptop) with each other to the extent not required.

However, at the same time, I love gizmos and you would find the latest ones with me. But their utility is limited as an equipment or a device, that's it.

This book is an attempt to express my gratitude towards what I have learned in the last 25 years and share it with you in a manner, which is implementable, in a simple way.

In this book, my commitment is to empower you with some amazing tools and techniques, which enhance your awareness. I am inviting you not to accept anything, which I share in this book unless you use and get the results. I don't want you to get loaded with some more knowledge; rather I wish to extract from you what you already have in mind related to time and transform it in an awareness which will work for you, not against you.

I have tried many things—attended many courses, read number of books on how to have more time for things which matters, but believe me what really worked for me is the most simple and basic thing- AWARENESS. Irony is that most simple things in life are usually overlooked.

With the help of awareness, along with some basic tools and techniques, I am consistently manufacturing time for myself. Let me share few results, which I have created over a period of time, which may inspire you and keep you hooked up till the end of this book:

- I take 4-6 vacations in a year, almost every alternate month.
- I am waking up at 4.45 am from almost last 10 years.
- I reach office by 8.15am and come back home by 6.30pm.
- We go for movie almost every week (usually on Fridays when it gets released).
- I write gratitude for 3 things in my journal (reflecting back yesterday) as first things in the morning and write 3 small wins when I retire for the day in night.

This I am following from last 7 years.

- I do at least one course either related to technical skill, behavioral skill or spiritual every year.
- I read/listen 1-2 books every month.
- I don't recall if I ever worked on Sundays since I started my company in 2005.
- I have never received complaint from any person that I didn't return back the missed call or I called up after a considerable delay.
- I check my mails maximum two times a day and that too the filtered list of mails by my Executive Assistant(EA).
- We have grown from 40 people to 130 people in less than 7 years.
- I plan and schedule all the important things in life on annual basis i.e. Holidays, Birthday, Anniversary, etc.
- In our office, if a person is required to sit late in office, he needs to take an approval by 5.30pm by mentioning the reason for late sitting.
- Our process and systems are super simplified, even a beginner can grasp with ease.
- Whenever there is escalation from a client about a person, instead of pointing finger at person we look at our system or process, which might have caused it and 8 out of 10 times we are proven right.

Are you impressed? At least a little bit? I can see a little smile coming on your face:)

As I shared earlier, the above results were accomplished through awareness of just one thing.

Want to know about it?

That's what the next chapter is all about.

1

CHAPTER

DISTRACT THE DISTRACTIONS!

> **Time is our most precious but non-renewable resource.**

Is it really possible to manufacture time?

Well..... answer is an emphatic yes..... if you know the secret recipe of doing so..... which I will be sharing in a while. For now, I would like you to imagine how your life will be if you are able to really manufacture time and have more time then you need in a day.

Imagine what all you would be able to accomplish in life.

Close your eyes and contemplate for a while.

Do this. Please.

You will thank me.

Okay.

Now I want you to consider this...

In the last 50 years, significant progress has been made in the field of time management. Numbers of books have been written and research is still going on to find the next best techniques of time management. There are number of workshops and seminars around this topic. Even big corporates spend huge money on this single issue in the hope to increase the productivity of their employees and also creating a work-life balance.

I guess, you might have also read few books or articles or may have attended few courses or seminars on this subject.

Have you been able to manage the time the way you want?

Ok, let me ask one simpler question—why do you want to manage time?

To have a work-life balance!

Right?

This makes me ask one more simple question—why do you want to have a work-life balance?

To do things which matters most at work and in your personal life!

Right?

If you are nodding in "Yes", why you have not been able to master the time management?

Should I tell you the reason?

Sure? Are you ready?

Ok, here it is:

"You should not manage time rather you should manage "distractions". If there is no distraction, time can be managed with ease and grace."

The immediate next question may come up in your mind—ok, I get this but I am back to square one! Now, instead of time, I need to get rid of distractions but how?

Don't worry! We have just started to scratch the surface.

I'll tell you how to deal with distractions.

Suppose, you are sent in a room, which is pitch dark and asked to push out the darkness from that room. Can you do that? Logically, it should be possible!

If you start fighting with darkness, is it going to solve this problem? Whatever you do to push the darkness, it would still be there but you may get tired. Now, instead of pushing the darkness, you just bring a candle in the room. Do you need to push the darkness any further? No!

Same is the case of distractions!

If you fight with distraction in the dark, it's not going to help; rather it will become stronger, leaving you weak and helpless. However, if you bring the candle of "awareness" in the darkness of "distraction", it just disappears.

Distraction is nothing but an absence of awareness!

The moment distraction disappears due to awareness; the time occupied by it also gets free. Now, the real challenge begins—what to do with this additional available time? This is where most people struggle even if the time is available. In 9 out of 10 times, this freed up time is usually occupied by another "distraction" which may not look like distraction in the beginning. You must be thinking that it will not happen in your case but believe me, it will.

Why?

Really interested to know?

Ok, let me share if you are insisting so much:-)

Absence of clarity or purpose for the free time always lead to another distraction.

It would be wise to discuss: what do we mean by the word "distraction"?

Distraction means diversion from the desired area of focus.

Distraction either reduces the available time for doing the important work or it takes more time to do that work. Distraction also leads to procrastination in the areas which are important for us.

Distraction can be present in one's life as an external distraction and internal distraction.

The external distractions can be in the form of social media Apps, TV, newspaper, video games, excessive use of gadgets etc.

Similarly, internal distractions can be mood, fatigue, feeling sleepy etc.

Just close your eyes for a moment and be present to the impact of distractions in your professional and personal life, specially the external distractions. It simply takes away your focus from the current work and does not add any real value in your life. It creates a vicious circle of constant pressure, urgency and not having time. The language of distracted person consists of words which are related to excuses or words loaded of self-pity.

Have you ever noticed that when you are distracted, time flies but if you are asked to be focussed, it appears that time has actually stopped.

Why does this happen?

Do you really want to know?

Ok, let me tell you—distraction provides an instant gratification and an easy escape from what really matters to you. However, in the long term, you experience pain, guilt and stress.

Have you experienced any itching or eczema on your skin, ever?

What do you do? You scratch it, right?

Come on, all of us have that urge and we have done that many time.

What do you experience after scratching?

Two things happens

1. You feel immediate relief.
2. The itching becomes more intense. Some people even scratch so much that they bleed!

Can you relate to the impact of distraction in your life now? This awareness is the key to create time, as much as you want.

You want an antidote to distraction?

Ideation is that antidote!

Let's start with Ideation, which is the first part of the time-manufacturing machine.

2

CHAPTER

IDEATION—MOTHER OF ALL HABITS!

> **A problem well stated is a problem half solved**

Spending time with oneself is the biggest source to manufacture time.

This statement may sound quite contradictory, isn't it?

You might wonder that instead of talking about how to manufacture time, I am asking you to spend time first (which you already lack), and that too with yourself.

Have you ever been to a village and seen people drawing water from a hand pump?

If not, you may just Google it and see how it works.

You would be surprised to know that to take out water from the hand pump, you first need to pour some water inside the hand pump. However, once it starts giving you water, you can take as much as you want.

Similar principle is applicable to create time. First, you need to invest some time to start manufacturing time.

The most basic and advanced tool to manufacture time is Ideation.

It is the foundation on which this whole technology of time manufacturing is based at. After reading this book, even if you implement just this one tool, you will experience at least 20X value of your time and money spent on this book.

If you observe closely, we attempt to spend time with almost everyone who is important in our life *i.e.,* office, parents, siblings, spouse, children, friends except one person- *oneself.*

When was the last time you sat with yourself without any distraction of mobile phone?

It's rare, right?

It's my commitment that by the end of this chapter, you'll start craving to spend time with yourself.

Let's first decode what ideation is. If you look at the dictionary meaning of word "ideation"—it means the formation of ideas or concepts.

It's an art and science of taking a step back and looking at the problem from outside which provides a different perspective. In spiritual world, it's also called witnessing. Attachment creates an illusion, which blind us from the solution.

You may recall any incident in your life when you were deeply involved in a mess or a problem and didn't get any solution but when you detached yourself from the problem, the solution just appeared.

Purpose of ideation is to create a space within yourself where an insight may enter and appear before you.

It's like taking a 30,000 feet view on a specified area of life which you are dealing with.

Ideation is quite confronting and uneasy in the beginning but once it comes in regular practice, it becomes effortless and automatic.

The next logical question may come in your mind: how to ideate and what to ideate upon?

I am sharing the most practical process of ideation:

1. Ideation notebook
2. When to ideate?
3. Where to ideate?
4. Duration of ideation
5. What to ideate upon?
6. How to ideate?
7. FAQs

1. Ideation notebook

Buy a smart notebook that has fine quality of paper. A separate notebook will help you to refer any ideation after some time. Further, it will keep your content private and confidential. In case, you are a techie or not in the habit of writing on daily basis, you may feel little overwhelmed while using this traditional way of recording your thoughts. But believe me, it is a highly effective tool. You may like to transfer it to your electronic device either by taking a picture or by typing it to the device or through speech to text dictation tool in your phone.

2. When to ideate?

Timing is very important for ideation. Morning time is the best time to ideate. Saturday morning or Sunday morning is the best to ideate.

3. Where to ideate?

The best place for ideation is a coffee shop near your home. Why coffee shop? For two reasons—one is that it's a kind of casual place and second, here you can get your favourite coffee and a comfortable environment. If you are a little of sophisticated kind, you may choose the coffee shop of any good hotel.

4. Duration and frequency of ideation

Your first ideation session may be little longer, say 60-90 minutes. However, your regular ideation session should be of minimum 30-45 minutes to get the real benefits. You should do ideation at least once in a week.

5. What to ideate upon?

Now, the next big question comes—what to ideate upon?

So, before the ideation routine, please make a list of important areas of your professional and personal life which are not working the way you want them to work.

Now, pick any important area and ideate upon it.

For example, if you are an entrepreneur and sales can be the area which is not working the way you want.

As per my experience so far, there are four important areas of life: Health, Wealth, Relationship, Spirituality. Wealth includes your career, business or any money matters. In the first ideation session, it's advisable to take up all these four (or more) important areas of life and just see what do you think about them.

6. How to ideate?

(a) Take out your phone, put it on flight mode and quietly slip it in your bag. Don't keep it in your pocket.

(b) If you are carrying any laptop or similar device, please don't take it out from your bag, let it be there.

(c) Now, take out your notebook and pen. Open up a fresh page.

(d) Choose a topic on which you want to ideate. You must choose a topic which is bothering you and consuming your mental energy *i.e.*, Investment, any office related issue, relationship not working etc. Mention the topic of ideation on the top of your notebook.

(e) Write this text: "What's going on in my mind related to...(mention the topic/issue name)

(f) Close your eyes for a minute and then start writing down whatever is coming in your mind related to your ideation topic. Don't judge yourself and keep writing. There should be minimum 5 points.

(g) Write this text: "How I can deal with it differently?"

(h) Close your eyes for a minute and then start writing down whatever is coming in your mind. Again, don't judge yourself and keep writing.

7. FAQs

(a) I am facing lot of resistance to think about any ideation topic.

This is the simple trick of our mind to keep us in the comfort zone of what we already know. You simply need to acknowledge this discomfort out of resistance.

(b) I feel blank when I think "How I can deal with it differently?" about an issue.

Here again, the mind is playing game with you. But if you sustain it for few minutes, you would be surprised to find the solutions which you can't even dream of. Mind is a very lazy servant☺

(c) I am having apprehension whether this tool will work for me as I think my problem is quite unique.

This is quite natural. We all think that our problems are unique but is it so in reality? I agree that few of our problems might be quite unique. However, I want to assure you that this tool works on all problems alike.

Don't give up on initial discomforts

You may face following situations during ideation:

1. You could not come up with any new insight related to the area which you have picked up for ideation.
2. Your mind was completely wavering here and there and you didn't feel like concentrating.
3. You felt utter boringness at the ideation process.
4. You felt that this is not my cup of tea, probably something else will work.

If you face any of the above symptoms or situations, please consider that ideation process is working for you.

Let me share my personal example to get more clarity.

In 2016, I finally decided to update our existing website which I was thinking of doing from last 3-4 years. Little did I know that instead of updation I'll end up making an altogether brand new website of Blue Consulting.

This 3-4 years of procrastination made this task even look much bigger than it actually was.

I clearly recall that it was early July'16 and I was sitting at Barista Café at Sector 18, Noida around 8.15 am. This is the only coffee shop in Noida which opens at 8am, so it perfectly suited me for the ideation.

That day weather was fantastic (in fact romantic) as it was raining. I ordered for my favourite Cappuccino and grabbed my favourite seat near the glass overlooking to outside. There was no other guest in the café that time.

I took out my red coloured ideation notebook and opened a fresh page for ideation on website of my company. I mentioned the date, time and location of ideation and also the topic: "New website of Blue Consulting by 30th September,'2016."

I vividly recall that I was very apprehensive about any positive outcome from this ideation process as I thought that this issue will take lots of time before I can even begin to start on website. It was creation of my own thought process.

The first things I did was to empty myself by writing down "What's going in my mind related to new website" I kept writing and must have written around 10-15 points *i.e.*, it will take lot of time, my other priorities will suffer, it's not urgent to take up right now, our website will require lot of content and who will write the content, will I'll be able to hire a good website designer/developer, content writer or who'll understand my requirements, etc.

The moment I finished writing, all the issues which were hovering in my mind, I felt an amazing relief as if a heavy thing has been lifted from my mind. This feeling inspired me to dig deeper in the ideation process.

Next thing that I did was to write down " How I can deal with it powerfully?". To my utter surprise, what I listed down just blew my mind with happiness. I just couldn't believe that the task which was occupying my mental space for such a long time seemed exciting and doable in three months.

I got a brilliant idea to mind map all the aspects related to new website. I was so excited that right after the ideation process (which took around 30 minutes), I downloaded a mind mapping App and mapped my mind completely. Yes, this is the mind map which I created that day:

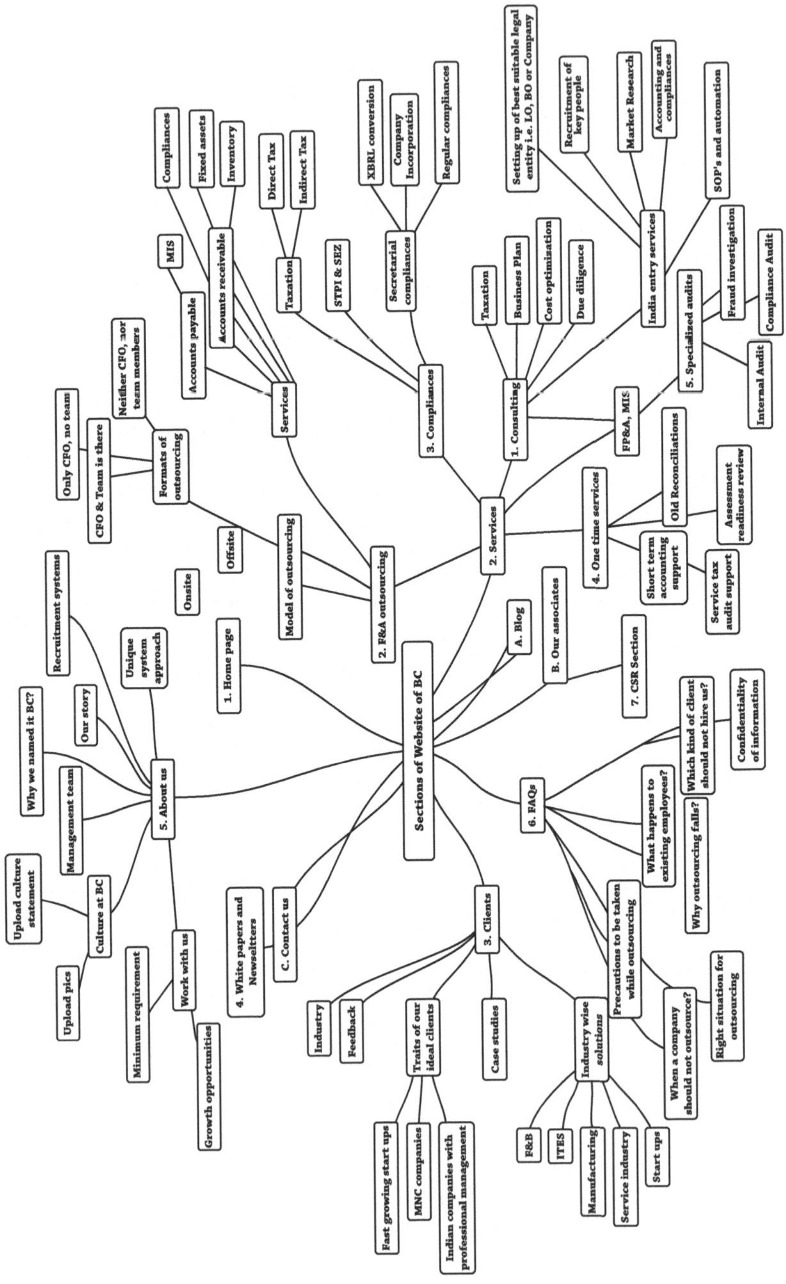
Sections of Website of BC
1. Home page
2. F&A outsourcing
Model of outsourcing
Onsite
Offsite
Formats of outsourcing
Only CFO, no team
CFO & Team is there
Neither CFO, nor team members
Services
Accounts payable
MIS
Accounts receivable
Compliances
Fixed assets
Inventory
Taxation
Direct Tax
Indirect Tax
2. Services
3. Compliances
STPI & SEZ
Secretarial compliances
XBRL conversion
Company Incorporation
Regular compliances
1. Consulting
Taxation
Business Plan
Cost optimization
Due diligence
FP&A, MIS
India entry services
Setting up of best suitable legal entity i.e. LO, BO or Company
Recruitment of key people
Market Research
Accounting and compliances
SOP's and automation
5. Specialized audits
Fraud investigation
Compliance Audit
Internal Audit
4. One time services
Old Reconciliations
Assessment readiness review
Short term accounting support
Service tax audit support
A. Blog
B. Our associates
7. CSR Section
6. FAQs
Which kind of client should not hire us?
Confidentiality of information
What happens to existing employees?
Why outsourcing falls?
Precautions to be taken while outsourcing
When a company should not outsource?
Right situation for outsourcing
3. Clients
Industry
Feedback
Traits of our ideal clients
Fast growing start ups
MNC companies
Indian companies with professional management
Case studies
Industry wise solutions
F&B
ITES
Manufacturing
Service industry
Start ups
4. White papers and Newseltters
C. Contact us
5. About us
Recruitment systems
Unique system approach
Our story
Why we named it BC?
Management team
Culture at BC
Upload culture statement
Upload pics
Work with us
Minimum requirement
Growth opportunities

Fast forward, on 3rd October'2016 (almost 3 months from the date of ideation) our new website went live and it turned out to be much better than what I had first imagined. I enjoyed every minute which I spent on this project. You know what- I created 100% of the content for this website on my own.

This is just one example. Whenever I have stuck in any area of my life, ideation has helped me the most. It generates some amazing ideas and more importantly, it brings back my focus on the subject which either I was avoiding or not getting time to look into it.

Once you bring focus on anything, clarity start emerging gradually. Doing anything with clarity takes much less time and produces more results.

However, any ideation without execution is an illusion.

Two other tools, which I am going to discuss in next chapters, helped me to put my ideation into action.

3

CHAPTER

SCHEDULING

> **"It doesn't require much strength to do things, but it requires great strength to decide what to do."**

What comes in your mind the moment you hear the word "Scheduling"?

Don't think much and start writing whatever comes in your mind.

Don't proceed further, if you haven't written at least 10 words, it's very important to know how you relate to scheduling.

From where did these words come?

Experience, perception and conditioning, right?

Real learning comes from unlearning.

How we relate to something usually exists in language only and the words which we use to describe something, establish a relationship with that aspect of life. To change your relationship with certain aspects, just change the context and words.

Try this!

Look at the following words in the context of scheduling:

1. Wonderful tool to create time
2. Peace of mind
3. Clarity
4. Workability
5. Freedom
6. Success
7. Control
8. Focus
9. Quality
10. Action

Read them one more time.

Are you feeling powerful?

If you really want to learn how to manufacture time, scheduling is the key tool.

One question might be crossing in your mind— if scheduling is so powerful, why most of the people don't use it consistently or they find it so hard?

There are two reasons for this:

1. Relationship with scheduling is not correct.
2. Design of scheduling is faulty.

We have already covered the first reason in the beginning of this chapter. Now, let's talk about the second one.

Consider scheduling as a physical tool in a factory, manufacturing some product. If the design of the tool is faulty, it's going to create trouble in manufacturing of that product and you will not get the desired result. There are only three components of an effective scheduling tool through which you can generate as much time as you want, with complete peace of mind.

However, most of the people either use one, or maximum two components of scheduling, but the most important component is always missing. You are already familiar with two components quite well but performance of these two components completely depends on the first component.

Moreover, the way people use these two components is also very rudimentary, hence not workable and usually associated with stress and anxiety.

Are you ready to absorb the art and science of scheduling which works for you every time?

Trinity of scheduling

An effective scheduling has three components:

1. Capture tool
2. Calendar
3. To-do list

All these components are tightly integrated and will not work if any one of them is missing.

As shared earlier, majority of people uses the second and third component only whereas the most basic component of scheduling is usually missing which is capture tool.

What is capture tool and how to use it?

As the name suggests, it's a tool to capture your thoughts. It's like a parking place for your thoughts on which you need to work sometime in future. Sometime, ideas come as a flash of light and then go.

Have you ever experienced the 'too much on my plate" when you look at your To-do list or Calendar? If yes, it's simply because capture tool is missing from the equation of scheduling. When capture tool is absent, many things in your mind keep consuming your attention and hence lowering your productivity, which ultimately result in reduction of time.

Where to capture thoughts?

There are two options:

1. Paper note book
2. Mobile phone

Paper note book is a good tool to capture your thoughts but its availability with you may be an issue. As a substitute, a pocket diary and pen may also be kept.

The second option, which is my personal favourite as well, is your mobile phone because it's always available with you whenever a thought/task comes in your mind related to any work which needs to be done sometime in future, which may be as early as tomorrow.

So, how to use your mobile phone as a capture tool?

I am sharing about two Apps which I have identified and personally used as capture tool after doing experiments for more than 10 years.

Good news is that both of them are free!

The first one is Google Keep.

It's one of the best note taking tools I have come across and I have used it dedicatedly for almost 3-4 years. Why did I stop using it? Simply because, all those tasks got done and now I can easily manage them through my to-do list only. This is the real testimony of generating time when your capture tool becomes redundant.

The best feature of Google Keep is that you can access it anywhere any time, on your phone, on your computer or iPad. The data always remain safe and you need not to worry about the back up at all.

Another great capture tool is One Note.

I'll suggest you to use this tool as a capture tool only if you are already using it for your office purpose. If not, please skip it and use Google Keep.

Though Google Keep is very easy to use but if you face any issue, just watch any video on You Tube on "How to use Google Keep?".

The next step is to create some categories to park your thoughts.

1. Next action (Personal)
2. Next action (Office)
3. Someday may be (Personal)
4. Someday maybe (Office)
5. Reference

You may use a different nomenclature which best describes your requirement, but please don't go beyond 5 categories.

Simplicity is the key for any system to work.

I'll just explain the use of these five categories.

The first two categories with the prefix of "Next action" captures those work (office or personal)which you want to accomplish in next few weeks but not sure when, hence can't park them in "To-do" list or "Calendar".

The third and fourth categories with the prefix of "Someday may be" captures those work or ideas on which you want to work someday when you have time and resources but these are very close to your heart.

For example, in my case, I want my company Blue Consulting to become a six Sigma certified company someday. Similarly, I had earlier parked a 10 days' Vipassana meditation in "Someday may be (Personal)" category which got recently completed.

The fifth category "Reference" captures those thoughts which keeps hovering around your mind and may come handy for reference, when required. For example, some news you read somewhere which you would like to access sometime in future, any unusual name of an author or personality which you keep forgetting etc.

Capture tool will be required at the time of weekly scheduling when you will take out some work from the "Next action" category and put them in either "Calendar" or "To-do" list.

Calendar

"Calendar" is used as equivalent to "scheduling" by many people, especially in the corporate world. To a greater extent, there is some truth as well. But here we'll use calendar just as one component of scheduling and not as substitute of it.

Which calendar App should be used?

In today's time, I find Google Calendar as the best App for managing calendar. It has many good features over the native App of your phone or laptop. However, if you are already using any other calendar App and find it convenient, please keep using as it's not going to make much difference when it comes to scheduling.

What's the use of Calendar?

It helps in managing your day and week with ease.

3 basic principles to get maximum results from calendar:

1. Schedule only those tasks which require more than 30 minutes.
2. Keep a breathing gap of at least 30-60 minutes between two tasks in calendar.
3. Never schedule more than 4 tasks in calendar.

If you just practice these three basic principles, you are sorted. These principles may look simple but if you practice them consistently, you'll be amazed by their powers and results.

Now, I am going to share with you a hack which will skyrocket your productivity and fire up your energy for the whole working day.

Ready to grab it?

It's this: The first task on your calendar should be the one which you are resisting the most.

I repeat because it's so important: The first task on your calendar should be the one which you are resisting the most.

This is where the real growth is hiding. This small step will multiply your productivity, satisfaction and confidence—all in one go.

Let's do a small exercise to experience what I am trying to share with you.

Read the following texts and close your eyes:

Step 1: Just imagine about any work-related task which you are resisting the most or procrastinating for a long time.

Step 2: Now, I want you to visualise and feel the emotions considering that you have completed that work as per your expectation. Feeling and emotions on completion of task are the most important.

Close your eyes and do this exercise even if it looks weird.

Warning: Don't move before doing this exercise.

What did you feel or experience?

I am sure you must have felt a sense of satisfaction and accomplishment or any other ecstatic emotions.

Now, just visualise that if you start experiencing this emotional state on daily basis, how life would be? No doubt, lot of resistance would come up but you can easily overcome just by focussing on the feeling and emotions which you will experience after doing that work. This strategy is inspired from a famous book of *Brian Tracy: Eat That Frog*.

This strategy of calendar setting process is going to manufacture the largest quantity of time in your life and will also bring the highest level of happiness.

Now, the bonus time!

I am sharing some bonus insights to make your calendar setting process a sure-shot success:

1. Protect the time blocked during the first half of the day as this is the time when you are most creative and energetic. I would suggest to keep your meetings in the second half or at least starting from 12 PM.
2. When you block a slot on your calendar, relate to it fully. It's like making an appointment with yourself and keeping it.
3. Always start your calendar scheduling with two weeks in hand. Many a time, when office work is going at peak or very hectic, you will feel tempted to pack everything in one week because when we schedule, we don't consider many unknown factors or situation which may come up.
4. Be happy about what you accomplished at the end of the day rather than being upset about what could not be done.

To-do list

Now comes the last component of the scheduling- To-do list.

This is the oldest way of scheduling and almost everyone is familiar with it. Even I remember using it during my study days as well.

Just like Calendar, effectiveness of "To-do list" is determined by the way how you use it.

Firstly, let's discuss where to maintain the To-do list. My

strong recommendation is to maintain the To-do list on your mobile phone for the simple reason that it's accessible when you need it. However, if you are already maintaining the To-do list in paper form or any other digital format which is working for you, please continue with that and just follow some basic principles and strategies which I'll be sharing in further.

All the smart phones comes with a built in "To-do list" App. However, I would strongly recommend not to use it because it's not very user-friendly, hence inconvenient.

I must have tried multiple Apps to maintain my "To-do list" but nothing comes closer to Swipes. I am using this App successfully from last 6 years. It's really simple to use and the best part is that its look and font is very sleek. As the name suggests, you can swipe a task to mark it as complete or schedule it for another time and day. There are three sections in this App:

1. Tasks not scheduled for today
2. Tasks scheduled for today
3. Tasks which got completed

To master this App, just watch a video on YouTube on "How to use Swipes" which is of 1-2 minutes duration and then you are good to go.

So this was about the tool to maintain the "To-do list".

Now, lets' talk about how to schedule the "To-do list" to enhance its effectiveness by 10X.

First, I'll talk about the categories to park your tasks and then I'll share the actionable hacks and strategies.

Your "To-do list" should have three categories:

1. Success list
2. Trivial list
3. Personal list

As the name suggests, "Success list" should have those tasks which are really important to do i.e. to check with a client about meeting in this week, agreement to be renewed, organize a strategic session with your team, etc.

"Trivial list" will carry those tasks which are trivial in nature i.e. send some basic information to a colleague, submit your expense statement for reimbursement, call people whom you promised to call back, etc.

"Personal list" will have those tasks which are personal in nature i.e. change address in your bank account, call a mechanic to fix something at home, etc.

Some do's and don'ts

Dos':

1. Use recurring reminders for tasks which are periodic in nature. For example, I used to read a Warren Buffett letter to its shareholders every Sunday, so this was a weekly recurring task in my to-do list.
2. When you are busy or receive a call and tell the person that you will call back in whatever time, just park it in your to-do list. It just takes less than 10 seconds to park a task 'call to be made'.

Don'ts:

1. Don't mention more than 7-10 tasks during a day. It feels very good when your to-do list is light. Even

if the work which you want to park additionally may take a minute or two, but quantity also matters because of our conditioning. So, even if you have completed your work as per calendar and could not do the task in your to-do list (which are four or five in numbers still left), you might be left with a feeling of little regret.

2. Don't fall in love with to-do list; rather get married to your calendar.
3. Don't set reminder (which rings a sound) in your to-do list except if it's very critical, for example for taking medicine at a specific time. The reason of not putting reminder is that they will unnecessarily distract you from your schedule (calendar) which is the most important for you.

   In case you need to set reminder in to-do list, please do so around the time when you are least productive or not able to maintain focus, for example-before or after-lunch time, going for a meeting (use the travel time). You may notice that doing the tasks in you to-do list doesn't require much energy or enthusiasm.

Some common pitfalls related to To-do list which you must be aware of:

1. When you start your to-do list, you would be tempted to park as many tasks in the first week itself, but I would suggest you to reduce your to-do list by at least 1/3rd of whatever you wish to plan to achieve.

   You might wonder that instead of motivating you to achieve and plan more, I am rather asking you to reduce the quantity. It's because when we start planning our to-do list, we always take the best case scenario and not able to account for our mood swings during the day, loss of willpower or any urgent work coming up which eats up a lot of time.

2. Another pitfall of to-do list is the feeling of not being able to complete all the tasks or being overwhelmed or deferring the tasks three or four times. You should not be guilty about not being able to tick off or swipe of all the tasks, rather you should be patting your back and celebrating the tasks which you could do successfully.

What should be scheduled first?

Let me tell you a story first!

Once there was an old professor who was about to retire from the college. He was very popular among students for his simple but practical advice.

He wanted to share his most important message to his students but was not finding a way for this. Finally, after lots of experiments, he found a good way to share his most important life message.

He invited some of his students over evening tea at his home. After tea was served and they had some casual conversation, the professor pull out four things below the table and put them on the table. One big glass jar, some rock pieces, some pebbles and some sand.

Students got really curious and excited by looking at these unusual stuff but knowing their professor, they could sense that he wants to share something valuable to them.

The professor got up from his chair and stood behind the table where this stuff was kept. He said time is the great equaliser in life and we all get 24 hours in a Day, 7 days in a Week and 52 weeks in a Year.

Who knows how many years we have left!

But we all know that how you choose to spend your time, will determine if your life will be fulfilling, satisfying and happy.

He said this empty jar represents your life and the time you have to fill.

The sand represents all the little things that really don't matter i.e. phone games, unnecessary YouTube videos, gossiping, etc.

He poured all the sands in the jar which filled up the jar to an extent.

The pebbles represent the things that matter a little i.e., casual hobbies, spending time out of compulsion, overtime at job or business etc.

Then he took pebbles and started filling them in the jar which filled up the jar almost to the half.

Then he pointed towards rocks and said, "These represent the important things in life which money can't buy i.e. health, family, friends, fighting for a cause, spiritual growth, etc."

He picked up rock pieces and started putting them in the jar one by one but could not fit in more than 2-3 pieces as there was no space left in the jar.

He further said, "When you choose to fill your time with the little things first, then you are left with no time for the important things in life".

However, when you give time to the IMPORTANT things FIRST, you'll be amazed at what you can accomplish.

To demonstrate this, professor emptied the jar by putting all things back at their respective places.

This time, in the empty glass jar, he put all the rock pieces one by one which filled the jar. He asked the students if jar is full. As it was quite visible that jar was full of rocks, students replied in unison- "yes".

At this reply, professor picked up the bowl of pebbles and started putting them one by one in the jar and these pebbles got settled around the empty spaces of rocks. When all the pebbles were there in the jar, professor asked once again if the jar is full. This time few students said "yes" and many kept mum as they were not sure about their answer.

Now, the professor picked up the bowl full of sand and started pouring it in the jar. Majority of the sand got settled around the small gap between rocks and pebbles. Still, around 10-15% sand got left.

The professor turned towards the students and said, "Who cares if some small and insignificant things doesn't fit in an enriched and fulfilled life".

You can clap if you liked the story:-)

Our association with scheduling is usually related to 'office work". However, scheduling is a tool which is helpful in leading a fulfilled life. We all know theoretically that work is just one part of our life and there are other important areas like health, relationship, spiritual journey, etc.

It's easy to lose focus on the important things in your

life and to fill the precious time you do have with things that don't mean a damn thing. Prioritising your time is critical to having a "full-filled" life. If you start with all the small and trivial things, you'll have no time for the things that really matter. BUT, if you give time to the things that are important first - not only do you have time for them, but also you'll find you have time for a whole lot more.

In her classical book *Top five regrets of dying people,* author *Bronnie Ware* compiled the top five regrets of people who were in the last phase of their life. Bronnie was an Australian nurse who spent several years' working in palliative care, caring for patients in the last 12 weeks of their lives. When she questioned her patients about their regrets in life or how they could have lived differently, following common points were repeated again and again:

1. I wish I'd had the courage to live a life true to myself, not the life others expected of me.
2. I wish I hadn't worked so hard.
3. I wish I'd had the courage to express my feelings.
4. I wish I had stayed in touch with my friends.
5. I wish that I had let myself be happier

When you think "scheduling" think of it as a tool to achieve anything you want in any important areas of your life including office work.

When you start scheduling on weekly basis, first think about what you need to get done in this week related to all important areas of your life i.e. relationship, health, wealth management, strategic office work etc. Now, whatever time is left, please plan your other work around it.

It may sound quite motivational, but difficult to practice. Believe me, it's much easier than you think and it's very fulfilling. In fact, when you start using scheduling this way, you will experience a lot of fulfilment in your office work as well.

Do it yourself- now!

You already have huge knowledge about lots of things in life but that doesn't help unless you put that knowledge into practice, right?

So, I don't want to leave you here just with the knowledge of scheduling, but I want you to experience it so that you get in touch with its real power.

Please don't proceed further in this book without doing scheduling. The best time to do this is NOW! In case, it's not possible right now, please do it when you pick up this book again.

Ready to experience the adventure of scheduling?

Let's begin!

Find a comfortable place where you will not be disturbed for next 30-45 minutes. Just get three things:

1. A note book
2. A pen
3. Your smart phone

Now, close your eyes for a minute and watch your breath which is coming and going through nostrils. Pay attention when it's coming to and going from nostrils.

Open your note book and start writing all the pending tasks which come to your mind. The tasks may be related to any category i.e. ,personal or office. They may be small or big. Just keep writing and don't think how you will do it. If you have any doubt whether it's a task worth mentioning, assume it's worth mentioning and write it down.

Your mind may like to stop writing after 10-15 tasks but keep thinking and writing. Just consider that you got a genie which will do all these tasks but for that you need to list all them down.

You should have at least 25 tasks which are pending and there is no limit on maximum numbers. If your list has not reached the minimum threshold of 25 tasks, keep thinking and writing. You also need to write down your wish list i.e. 10 days' meditation retreat, 15 days' bike tour with friends etc.

Are you done?

Now, stop for a minute and feel your emotional state.

The step you just completed is the most important step in the scheduling process. Till the time, you don't know what is pending and how much is pending, how would you schedule and accomplish?

I am sure, you might be feeling quite relaxed because you have just emptied your mind for the first time, it's an amazing feeling, isn't it?

Now, you need to categorise them as per the categories made in your capture tool i.e. Google Keep:

1. Next action (Personal)
2. Next action (Office)
3. Someday may be (Personal)
4. Someday maybe (Office)
5. Reference

Now, start putting a category at each pending task of the list in your notebook. You may also use some acronyms i.e. NAO for Next Action (Office) category or SMO for Someday may be (Office). Don't worry about putting the wrong category. If you want to refresh your memory about the purpose of each category, just go to the capture tool text and review it.

Go through your list once again and see if you want to keep all the tasks and also review the categories allotted to these tasks.

After doing review, start parking the tasks under the relevant category of your capture tool.

Congratulations!

Just relax and pat your back for taking this great step in creating huge time for yourself.

Now comes the action time!

The tasks categorised in Capture Tool need to be scheduled in Calendar and To-do list for execution.

Before you start scheduling your tasks in Calendar or To-do list, brush up the following points once again:

1. Only those tasks will be scheduled in Calendar which will take 30 minutes or more to complete i.e. Dinner party at friend's home, annual vacation, parents' anniversary celebration, proposal making, research on some topic, review of salary, etc.
2. Schedule only 50% work time on your Calendar and keep the remaining as open. So, if you work day is of 9 hours, don't schedule more than 5 hours.

3. There shouldn't be more than 4 tasks in your Calendar.
4. First task on your Calendar should be something which you are resisting the most and it is very important i.e. Preparing a long pending report which requires some research, revision of HR policy as per the inputs of last 3 town hall meetings.
5. Your To-do list should not have more than 7-10 tasks during the day and none of them should take more than 30 minutes. Usually, these tasks takes 5-10 minutes to complete i.e. Call a client for meeting, send a book as gift to a friend through Amazon, write a mail to client for renewal of agreement, etc.

   Now, open your Calendar, pick up the tasks from your capture tool and schedule them. Similarly, open your To-do list, pick up the tasks from your capture tool and schedule them.

When to do scheduling?

Do your scheduling on weekly basis, either on Sunday or first thing on Monday morning. If you are an early riser, please do the scheduling in the morning time as first thing because that time you would be fresh and creative. Get a fresh cup of your favourite tea or coffee and play some soothing music. If you are at a place which is overlooking to a garden, it will add in your creativity. Initially, the weekly scheduling might take 30-45 minutes to schedule and after some time it will come down to maximum of 15-20 minutes.

When you finish your workday, just check how much

you could complete today out of the scheduled tasks and celebrate that. Never focus on what you didn't accomplish.

So, what to do with the tasks which you didn't complete today?

Reschedule these tasks to some other day during the week to the extent possible or put them back to capture tool so that you can reconsider them when you plan your next week from the capture tool.

In addition to weekly scheduling, it's very important that you spend 5-10 minutes every morning to go through your Calendar and To-do list for the current day tasks. It may happen that one of the meetings scheduled today might have been postponed or you'll not be attempting some small tasks in your To-do list.

Scheduling is a habit

Scheduling is nothing but a habit which, if practised for a certain time regularly, becomes automatic. Just relate the habit of scheduling with your other habits which you learnt over a period of your life and which were not easy and not possible without regularity, for examples-cycling, learning to write, learning to walk, driving. Now, after learning these habits, do we have any question about how do we do these things or we ever question whether the intended benefit will accrue or not? Same is with scheduling.

First we create our habits and then our habits create us.

Initially, scheduling may not be easy and you may find it very mechanical or boring but don't give up and always remember these lines:

1. Discipline or regret, both are painful and you always have a choice to choose.
2. Price of discipline is always less than the price of regret.

   Once you understand that objective of scheduling is to bring work ability, joy, happiness, time to take care of your health and hobbies, then you will be inspired to bring regularity in your scheduling. You should be doing scheduling with a happy state of mind rather than as a compulsion.

Never schedule a task which you can delegate or outsource

You need to ask the following question every time when you park any tasks in Capture tool or when you schedule the tasks in your Calendar or To-do list:

Can I delegate or outsource this task?

If you get the answer in "Yes", park this task in your "To-do list" so that you can delegate or outsource during the day or week.

There is a small flow chart which will help you to decide which tasks should be delegated or outsourced:

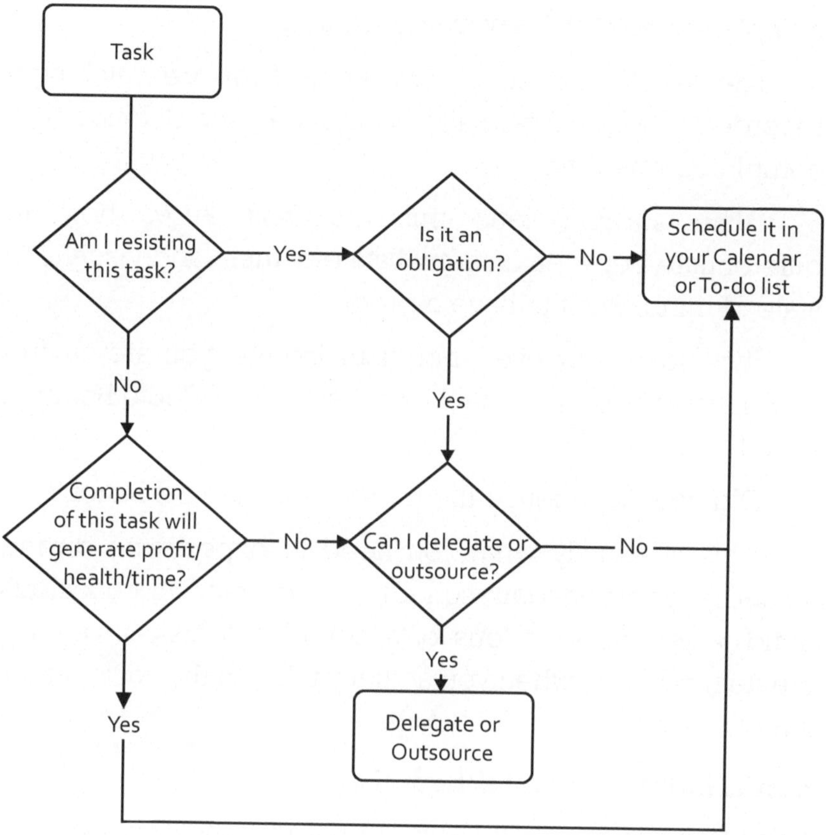

Role of visualisation in scheduling

Visualisation has immense benefits in getting the work done which you have scheduled. There are many ways of visualisation and lots of techniques are available. However, we are mainly talking about how visualisation can help in scheduling and let me share how to do the visualisation.

Once you are done with your daily review of Calendar and To-do list in the morning, just close your eyes and start visualising your emotional state of mind considering that the tasks which you had scheduled for the day are getting completed exactly the way you wanted.

The visualisation should be like as if you are watching a recorded movie wherein all the tasks on your Calendar got completed one by one.

The subconscious mind doesn't know how to differentiate between an actual state of mind and visualised state of mind. Want to have a proof?

Just close your eyes and visualise that you are having your favourite food or snacks i.e. Pani Poori, Chole Bhature, Aloo Kachori.

Did you experience the mouth-watering sensation?

This is exactly what you need to experience during visualisation of your daily schedule. Once your subconscious mind tastes the emotions of a completed task, it doesn't create hindrance when you actually take up that task, rather it motivate you.

Bonus habit : Annual scheduling

This is one of the most powerful habits in scheduling. The best time to do annual scheduling is at start of the calendar year or financial year and the second best time is - NOW!

Yes, you read it right! You can do your annual scheduling at any point of time during the year. Just consider the whole year from that particular month in which you do the annual scheduling. For example, if you decide to do the annual scheduling in the month of October'2019, then consider the period from October'2019 to September' 2020.

In my case, the best part of annual scheduling is planning for vacations during the year. I usually sit with the office holiday calendar to know the long weekends. In addition to vacations, I also plan the following:

- My birthday
- My wife's birthday
- Our marriage anniversary
- One spiritual retreat

Annual scheduling puts you at the driver's seat and you feel empowered.

> ***"If You Don't Have A Well Maintained Schedule, Then You Are Attending Stuff Or Doing Things As Per Somebody else's Schedule Or Priorities"***

4

CHAPTER

DEEP DIVE SESSION

> **Consistently repeated daily actions +Time=Unconquerable results.**

Deep dive session is the Brahmastra (the ultimate tool) of all the tools, which I've discussed or will be discussing throughout this book for manufacturing time.

However, this tool can only be used once you have mastered the Ideation and Scheduling.

Please pay additional attention to get hold of this important tool.

Let's go back to your childhood when you were in school.

Do you recall the experiment of burning paper through a piece of glass, which you need to hold still under the sun.

Wasn't that amazing?

However, will the paper catch fire if you keep moving the glass?

No, right?

The same analogy holds true in case of our focus and attention on important work. Even if you had some amazing insights during ideation process and you have scheduled very well (almost the way I explained in the last chapter), still you won't get that exponential result if deep dive session is missing from the trinity of your time manufacturing tools.

What is a deep dive session?

It's a 60 minutes session dedicated on any important area of your life wherein you don't access your phone or check any mails on your computer or laptop or any electronic device.

Why deep dive session is so critical?

Did you notice that I have used the word *critical* instead of important or urgent. If you observe closely, your attention span on anything doesn't last more than 10-15 minutes. Even if you are working on an ultra urgent proposal but still you get carried away by your habit of checking phone at intermittent period of 10-15 minutes. If you make a list of what did you work on whole day, the quantity of work may be huge but quality and relevance would be very minimal.

I have a habit of reading autobiographies of successful people and I might have read more than 50-60 autobiographies which relates to diverse areas i.e. business, sports, acting, singing, diplomats, politician etc. One thing, which I found common among all these great personalities, is their ability to work with undivided attention on something in which they excelled in life.

You might think that these types of people were born genius or maybe you don't want to work that hard. It's a complete misconception. In today's time, you can learn almost any skill if you work on it consistently. Further, it's a very big misbelief that these types of people worked hard. Ok, you tell me one thing- when you watch 4 to 5 episodes of any new release on Netflix or Amazon Prime, did you work hard or rather you enjoyed it. You enjoyed it, right?

One more reason of why you need deep dive session technology is that it will become the single most differentiating factor in your success.

Ask me how?

Simply because your competition is engaged in shallow or trivial work.

Just imagine what would become possible if you start doing just 5 deep dive sessions every week on something which you want or need to excel and resisting it currently. It culminates into approx. 20 deep dive sessions every month and whopping 240 sessions in a year.

One deep dive session of just 60 minutes per weekday is quite easily manageable and you can increase its frequency if your schedule allows it. In fact, when I started practising deep dive session around 5 years ago, I also started with a target of 5 such sessions per week but now I average almost 8-10 such sessions every week.

Now, I am addicted to deep dive session and it will happen with you as well. It's the world's best addiction with no side effects, only great benefits:)

Some do's and don'ts when you start your deep dive session

Do's:

1. If possible, start your day with the deep dive session on your calendar.
2. Pick up the area, which you are resisting the most.
3. Keep working on the subject even if you don't feel like doing it. Your mind will lure you every possible way from the deep dive session but you need to be aware and continue.

Don'ts:

1. Don't use your mobile phone even once during the deep dive session. Keep it on airplane mode or silent and slide it into your bag or drawer where you can't see it.
2. Don't use Internet if your work doesn't require it. However, if it requires use of Internet, please close your e-mail application before you start.
3. Don't take any break except a stretch break of 60 seconds after 30 minutes.

Test the technology

You might be feeling a little bit overwhelmed after reading this chapter. So, I would advise you to stop here and test with one deep dive session, either today or latest by tomorrow before picking up this book again.

If you have trusted me so far, just do it!

However, if you are convinced about the deep dive sessions, you may continue with this book but I would still suggest you to experience it before proceeding further.

My experiences of deep dive sessions

I always get goose bumps while sharing about what I got from deep dive sessions. I can talk about it for hours with the same interest. Let me try to share some of my experiences concisely so that you get the context:

1. **Website of Blue Consulting:** If you recall, I shared about how I mind mapped the content of new website of Blue Consulting (the company which I co-founded) through ideation tool. Once I did that, the next challenge was to convert it into reality. That's where deep dive sessions worked magic. I started scheduling deep dive sessions every week to execute the new website. The 60 minutes of undivided attention during deep dive sessions helped me to create some amazing content for the website. I invested approx. 30-40 deep dive sessions across 3 months period to complete the content and other aspects. I can still feel the emotions when our website went live and got amazing reviews from client and friends. This was in July-Sep'2016.
2. **Profile updation:** We are in August'2018 and our latest company profile was made in 2012. After that, we kept making some small changes but base was almost same which didn't reflect the journey we had in these 6 years. If you have ever attempted to create a company profile, you might understand the difficulties I am talking about. Creation of a new profile requires some deep thinking and kind of out of the box approach as you would like to create something distinct. Deep dive sessions helped me

create a profile, which exceeded even my own expectations. I invested approx. 8-10 sessions to create a brand new contemporary profile.

3. **Opportunity Australia:** Somewhere in the mid of 2016, I got an idea to look at overseas market for offshoring opportunities related to the services which we were providing in the domestic market. We had grown to a decent size of 105 people and thought it's an appropriate time to take some calculated risks to tap lucrative opportunities. Having an idea was one thing and putting it in action was an altogether different thing. Most of the ideas fail because of no execution or poor execution. I kept pondering on this idea but never dared to put it into execution.

   Then, in September'2017, I finally decided to give it a fair shot. Again, I took help of deep dive session technology for execution of this idea. In two months' time, I carried an in-depth research about three markets i.e. USA, UK and Australia and we finally selected Australia to test the opportunity. I declared the date of my visit to Australia, which was in first week of March'2018 and booked my tickets as well. Now, I had 4 months in hand to look for relevant contacts in Sydney. When I started to work on this idea, I didn't know even a single person in Australia but as I made progress through dedicated deep dive sessions, the clarity started emerging and just one week before leaving for Sydney, I had 22 confirmed meeting and 30 tentative meetings. I was there in Sydney for 3 weeks and out of total 15 working days, I did 46 meetings. Though, we didn't pursue offshore market further as we could clearly see that we should focus on India only, but I have huge satisfaction that I could convert my idea into reality.

4. **Simplification of MIS:** I am a big fan of simplified processes. The word "simple" sounds easy but it's not. In fact, it's quite easy to complicate things but very difficult to simplify.

   On my journey at Blue Consulting, I created MIS of my direct reportees and over a period of time these MIS became complicated and kind of redundant to reflect the current realities. I guess, this happens with all of us at different stages of life. We create something and then forget to question its relevance.

   So, in March'2019, I decided to review the MIS of all my direct reportees including my own MIS. I scheduled deep dive sessions for this and to my amazement, within a week I could simplify all of them to the extent that these MIS now only takes just 25% of the time to prepare as compared to earlier MIS and 200% more relevant.

5. **Structuring of database:** One of the most important part in any sales and marketing strategy is an accurate and updated database. Over the period since we started in 2005, we have accumulated a huge database of existing and potential clients. Though we use one of the best CRMs to manage our database but the current structure and staleness of our database was bugging me from last 2-3 years and I was kind of ignoring it mindfully. During an offsite ideation trip along with my business partner,

I picked up this as an issue to be addressed, before we create or revise our sales and marketing strategy. This was in February'2019. After coming back, I was quite confident that I'd address this issue in a very short time through deep dive sessions. I was proven wrong. It took almost 2-3 times more than what I had initially thought of. However, the kind of satisfaction that I got after getting it done was mind blowing. It steered my confidence to a new height.

6. **Activation of CRM features:** When I was working on database, I realized that we are using just 10% of the functionality of our CRM. Initially, I thought that it will take 3-4 deep dive sessions and I'll configure it to the optimum level. Just like in case of database, it took much more time than what I had planned. The advantage of going deep is that you get to know lot of issues which are associated or connected and were kind of hidden earlier. For example, we were using a different software for e-mails and were quite happy with its performance. However, while exploring the features of our CRM, I got to know that we can send e-mails much faster directly from our CRM which saved huge efforts and time.

7. **Warren buffet's letters to shareholders:** Long back, I had heard an audio book on *Warren Buffet-Tap Dancing to Work* wherein the author mentioned about an amazing habit of this maverick investor. When Warren Buffet started Berkshire Hathaway, he also started writing a detailed letter to its shareholders in which he talked about the business in detail along

with his thought process on some complicated topics i.e. value investment, role of depreciation on profit, nuisance of some accounting concepts. The habit, which he started in 1965, is continued till date. In 2016, I decided to read all of his letters to shareholders till date. I visited the website of Berkshire Hathaway and couldn't believe the utter simplicity of the one of the most richest men in the world. On the home page of www.berkshirehathaway.com, there was a link of "Warren Buffet's Letters to Berkshire Shareholders". On the website, these letters are hosted from 1977 onwards. I scheduled one deep dive session every Sunday and in less than 50 weeks I read all 41 letters. I still can't believe that I have gone through such a treasure of knowledge in such a short period of time.

I would be eager to hear from you about your accomplishments through deep dive sessions. You can mail me at cgoyal.bc@gmail.com.

Happy deep diving!

5

CHAPTER

TIME CREATION HABITS

> **"Time is the force that magnifies those little, almost imperceptible, seemingly insignificant things you do every day into something titanic and unstoppable."**

Congratulations for learning the trinity of time creation technology. All my current habits of time creation are a direct result of Ideation, Scheduling and Deep dive session.

Now, I am sharing some time creation habits, which you can start immediately. Let me tell you something in advance: you will resist applying them because little voice in your mind will say that it's not possible in your case as your work or business is different than mine. This is where you need to say to your little voice- ok, I get it but let me just try it for sometime and I'll leave it if it doesn't work in my case.

So, fasten your seat belt as we are going to take off to discuss some amazing time creation habits in this chapter.

Habit–1 : Check e-mails only TWICE a day

Yes, you read it right, it's twice a day only! If you are employed or self employed, e-mail checking has become an automated habit. I have seen people refreshing their browser or mail App if they don't see any new mail when they open their e-mail account as if it can't happen. E-mail checking is one of the biggest distractions that keeps wavering your focus throughout the day and you never get time for deep dive session to work on important tasks.

I remember, it was early 2003, and I was heading the Finance & Accounts function at a Fortune 500 company. We used to have lot of trainings on various topics at regular intervals. One such training session was organised by our company's Managing Director. This session was with his close friend who was based in Singapore but visiting India during that time. He shared an efficient way of dealing with e-mails that he himself practised. His sharing can be summarized in following points:

- Disable the Auto refresh feature in the Outlook or any other e-mail App you use. Get your mails manually by pressing send/receive button.
- Never open your e-mails within 2 hours of reaching office. If your office time is 9am, open your e-mail not before 11am.
- Never check e-mails when you are about to leave office in the evening. There should be at least one-hour gap when you last check your mails and the time when you leave in the evening. So, if you leave office around 7pm, don't check your mails after 6pm.

- Check your mails only twice a day. However, if you need to send any urgent mail, you can do that in between as well but never pull back your new mails more than two times. The reason why I am insisting on checking your incoming mails twice is that you will be doing it in batches, which will keep you undistracted during the day. I have observed that if there is an important/urgent mail, the person may inform you by phone or message as well.

  Initially, it seemed difficult to follow this habit as we all managers were in a default habit of checking mails every now and then. However, when he made his point by stressing on the fact that if he can do it successfully in abroad in a business country like Singapore why can't we do it in India, I thought that I should at least try it for few days.

  To my pleasant surprise, it worked and it worked rather very well. I experienced almost 20-30% increase in my productivity and more than that my happiness quotient went up by many notches. Since 2003, I am following this golden rule suggested by him.

  I would like to add one more point, which I am practising with great success— don't access your office e-mails on your phone. It may sound very orthodox in today's hyper connected world, but believe me e-mails on phone is a great distraction, hence time consumer. Moreover, you are not even aware about it because you feel that faster response to e-mail is equivalent to being efficient.

Focus and consistency gets compromised heavily when you access e-mails on phone. If there comes an emergency to access your office e-mail, you may access it through browser mode in your phone. Why browser mode? Simply because it's inconvenient and it will demotivate you to access your e-mail frequently.

To follow above e-mail practices successfully, it's very important that you inform people about it gradually. Initially, people may not like it, specially your clients or seniors but they will start accepting it when they see huge improvement in your efficiency and work quality.

Habit –2 : PUSH the distraction and PULL the freedom

The most fundamental technique to create time is to configure all your electronic devices (especially your mobile phone and laptop) based on PULL feature. Let's take the example of your most used electronic device- mobile phone.

The standard setting on your mobile phone is usually based on PUSH feature wherein the information and content is pushed to your device automatically i.e. notifications, e-mails, ads etc. Initially, it sounds quite good to receive everything automatically but soon you get swamped away by the deluge of information which keeps you occupied and distracted. For that matter, even the calls from unknown number is kind of pushing information to you.

So, what to do?

Just do the opposite of PUSH, practice using PULL feature. You should pull the desired information whenever you need it. For example, when you have free time, you can manually refresh the e-mail to receive the new mails. Similarly, you can return all the calls in a dedicated time block of 15-20 minutes.

Habit–3 : Learn to say 'NO'

Usually, all of us have expertise in one habit - saying YES to people who are senior to us either in age or designation. It's quite an automatic response system. Many times we realise it the moment we utter YES but by that time the arrow has left the bow and can't come back.

Why does that happen when we don't even want to say YES?

It happens because of two chief reasons:

- We want to look good before people and also have a FOMO (Fear Of Missing Out).
- We are not scheduled.

Saying YES to everything creates pressure and it leaves less time available with you.

75% of this problem gets cured the moment you start scheduling. It becomes a lot easier to say NO without any guilt when you have clarity of your schedule, at least for a week. Research has found that people who say NO after a thoughtful consideration earns more respect than people who say YES without any thinking.

I'm not suggesting to start saying NO to everything which does not fit to your overall purpose or schedule, all I am suggesting is to learn to say NO after due consideration.

In case, you can't say NO in a situation, always buy some time to think over and get back. Believe me, people don't feel offended except in some cases where it's mainly because of certain personality traits. When you buy certain time to think over, you actually get to deliberate whether you can entertain a particular request or not. Even if you end up saying YES out of compulsion, the other person will get a clear message that you may not say YES easily next time.

This simple awareness will create some amount of time and contribute to your happiness.

Habit–4 : Simplify, Simplify & Simplify

When you buy any property, following three factors are very important for decision-making:

1. Location
2. Location
3. Location

No, it's not a typo error. Location has been mentioned three times to signify its importance.

Similarly, when it comes to creation of time, following three factors are very important:

1. Simplify
2. Simplify
3. Simplify

Dictionary meaning of the word *simplify* is to make something simpler or easier to do or understand.

Now, a little voice in your head might ask- but how come it's related to creation of time? When you simplify something that is easier to do or understand, you will save a lot of time. Time saved is equal to time created.

The best example of simplification is Uber App. Booking of a cab on Uber is just a child's play—it's like tap tap and done. You need to look into your life and see what you can simplify. The best way to start is to make a list of tasks, which you find, little complicated or time consuming. Go through each item on your list one by one and question the way it is done currently. You will be amazed to know that you were doing something because either you learned it that way and never questioned it or you were told to do it in a certain way and you thought this is the only way it should be done.

Let me give you an example. In my office, I designed a MIS for Admin function around 3-4 years ago and since then the same format was being followed. It used to take lot of time for the person to prepare it and also lot of time for me to review it. As a result, I had started avoiding reviewing it and used to skip it almost every alternate month. To tackle this problem heads on, I scheduled a deep dive session of 60 minutes to simplify the format. I was quite apprehensive when I started the session but by the end of the session I could create a format that now takes less than one fourth (1/4th) of time to prepare and one fifth (1/5th) of time to review, without compromising the internal controls.

After this experience, I schedule a deep dive session every month to look at what I can simplify further and every month I always get something to work on to simplify, however small it may be.

Remember: Time saved is time created.

Habit–5 : Hotel check in for ideation and deep dive sessions

This hack is one of the biggest and highly effective time creators, in one shot!

If you need to work on something very quickly and in a focused manner, just check in a good hotel or resort within a 50-100 kilometers of your residence for at least 2 nights, alone. Declare to your office that you will not be reachable for these 2-3 days and if possible keep your phone in a switched off mode. Alternatively, you may carry a new SIM and this number may be given to your family or one office colleague to address any urgency.

Your main agenda should be to ideate upon something very important and deep diving in it. It would be a good idea to go through the two chapters of this book on ideation and deep dive session before you check in so that you get clarity and necessary motivation.

The purpose of hotel check is to take your attention off from the usual place of work and home that becomes quite monotonous sometime. Fresh air of a new place allows new ideas to emerge in your mind. Further, you get a cluster of time blocks together that takes care of your usual pretense that you don't have sufficient time. This may sound quite easy but let me warn you, it's not. Simply because you are not habitual of thinking and doing work in such a focused manner where you have negligible distractions of work and home.

You would be having a plenty of time with yourself in these 2-3 days. You must attempt to achieve at least 12-15 deep dive sessions of 60 minutes in this time period. Just imagine your productivity level if you devote these many deep dive sessions on anything. This habit is practised by usually all the successful people and they consider it one of their most effective strategies to tackle anything in life.

Now, let's talk about some fun part of hotel check in. If your budget allows, I would suggest checking in at a very good hotel, which you consider expensive. This is a great opportunity to treat yourself well. Go for a spa session, enjoy drink in the pool or go for a long walk, have the best food etc.

I would advise to do hotel check in at least once in a quarter.

Habit–6 : Instant motivation

Have you ever felt low and demotivated?

I am sure you must have. What happens in that state?

You don't feel like doing anything, right? The confidence level goes down and negative things around life starts emerging before your eyes which works as a fuel to the fire of lowness or demotivation.

This kind of mental state is a big time guzzler. It's a vicious circle- you don't feel like doing anything and at the same time you feel guilty of doing nothing.

How can you come out of this state? What are the possible ways?

Just think about and your answers might come under following possible solutions:

1. You speak to a friend or someone you trust about it, which makes you light.
2. You do nothing during the day but when you get up after a good night sleep, the mind reboots itself and you feel better.
3. You engage yourself in any sports or something you enjoy doing which alters your mental state.

All the above solutions are good but time consuming, isn't it? Further, if you need support of someone else to come out of this state, then you are dependent on that person and he or she may not be available when you are in need.

How would it be if you could pull out yourself from this mental state on your own within few minutes?

It would be amazing, isn't it?

So, let me share two secret techniques that are very simple yet most people don't use it. Actually, simple things are mostly overlooked. Here you go— build your reservoir of instant motivation using these simple techniques:

1. **Wins:** Write down all the wins you had from childhood till date. Include everything which makes you smile and you are proud of, which can be related to academics, sports, habit, values, relationship, leadership, help. If you are not sure whether you should write a particular win or not, it means you must write it down. This list may go from 20 to 100 or more. Now, just go through this list from top to bottom with full emotions. How do you feel?

   This is your biggest instant motivation hack. Keep this list handy in your mobile phone so that you can access it whenever you need it.

2. **Videos:** I am sure you must have watched many videos till date which you really found inspiring and which also increased your confidence, at least for the time being. Now, if you had compiled the link of these videos over a period of time, you would have created an amazing playlist that can give you an immediate boost to your state of mind.

You can start this habit now and start compiling the list of most inspiring videos. I have created an amazing list of videos over a period of time in the Google Sheet and whenever I need instant motivation, I just watch one of them and my state of mind changes immediately.

If you want access to my list of videos, you can mail me at cgoyal.bc@gmail.com and I'll add you in the shared list.

Habit–7 : Pooch daala to life jhingalala!

If you could recall, Tata Sky came up with an interesting TV ad campaign and the central theme was "Poochne mein kya jaata hai- Pooch daala to life jhingalala" (There is no harm in asking- It makes your life rock!).

Around same time, I was also attending a six month long leadership program and in one of the sessions, our coach spent more than two hours on a magical word - ASK. She said that we operate in our life mostly through assumptions; we don't ask, rather we assume. She further asked-- do you ever realize that how skewed your assumptions can be? And then she shared many examples from her personal life.

Since that day onwards, *Pooch daala to life jhingalala* became my mantra of life. If I tell you percentage wise, in certain situations where I was about to assume something but I dared to ask, I was almost 70-80% time wrong. This I am talking about those instances where I actually asked but there might be many instances where I didn't ask and assumed on my own.

You might be wondering that though it's a good concept but how it is related to creation of more time in life. It is very much related to my dear friend. When you ask instead of assuming on your own, lot of re-work is avoided in life, which directly save huge amount of time.

For example, you had a brain-storming session of almost 4-5 hours with your client to create a business plan. Now, you start working on it and suddenly you stuck up on few things. You have two choices—either you assume or ask from client. If your assumptions are based on your understanding or memory and you spend considerable amount of time, there is a strong possibility of re-work when your client reviews the business plan. You might repent that you should have asked it before hand. However, if you ask there will be two outcomes—your assumptions get validated (and client may appreciate it) or client shares his version, which saves lot of time. In both cases, you don't lose anything.

Habit-8 : Declare an odd time before call or meeting

You must have experienced stretched calls or meetings, which make your schedule completely haywire and you can't say no but you sulk internally because of helplessness.

There is an easy solution that has been tried and tested many times successfully. In my case, the success rate is between 80-90%, which is quite good, isn't it?

The solution is- just declare an odd time at which either you need to leave for another meeting or need to attend another call. For example, your meeting time is from 3 to 4pm and considering your past experience you know that this meeting will surely stretch beyond the scheduled time without adding any value to the solution of problem. In such a case, you can tell at the beginning of meeting that you need to leave for an urgent meeting at 4.10pm.

This way, you have very politely informed the other person in advance. Further, when the meeting is half way, you may just remind the person that you would be required to leave at 4.10pm. This will have two immediate benefits: 1. You will get free by 4.10 or 4.20pm. 2. The discussion would be more specific due to time constraints.

You can apply the same solution when you have a scheduled call and you know that the call will get extended beyond the scheduled time.

Habit–9 : AIR sheet

This habit will save huge amount of time when you attend any seminar, workshop or training. I learned this amazing technique from my friend Anant Kasibhatla who is a memory coach and Limca Book record holder.

The learning of any seminar or training can be divided in three broad categories:

1. Actions which you need to take after the workshop(A)
2. Ideas which you can use (I)
3. References which you would be required to refer again (R)

   So, while making notes in the seminar or training, you can use the following format and keep mentioning the insights in the relevant box:

Name of the workshop/training

Date **Location**

Action	
Ideas	
Reference	

After completion of seminar or training, you can simply take a picture of this sheet and access it anytime anywhere. This simple habit has increased my efficiency of extracting more from any seminar or training. Further, it saves lot of time that used to go while searching for the notebook where I made notes of a particular seminar or training to find out a specific insight during the event.

Habit–10 : Hire an EA

EA means Executive Assistant. If you are an entrepreneur or at a CXO level role, EA is a must for you to create time. She can free up 30-60% of your time that you currently spend on administrative activities. The moment you read this last line, a defense statement will pop up in your head saying, I don't spend my time on administrative activities. It's simply because you don't consider them as administrative activities due to habit and conditioning over a period of time.

Before we proceed further, let's first talk about what are the administrative activities that you might be doing currently without awareness. The list I am sharing below is just an illustrative one and you may add activities based on your own experience:

1. Official e-mail checking and replying
2. Delegation and follow ups with your team
3. Personal works like school fee of kids, passport renewal, ticket booking etc.
4. Compilation of any information from internet
5. Managing your LinkedIn account
6. Co-ordination with client and vendors
7. Sending meeting invite and managing calendar
8. Preparation of any report or basic level of analysis
9. Attending your calls when you are in meeting

The bottom line is that as an entrepreneur or CXO, every minute of your official time should be spent on strategy, vision and growth of business.

You may not feel comfortable having an EA because of following possible reasons:

1. It will cost you extra money.
2. You need to spend extra time to train the EA.
3. Apprehension of losing touch with your team.
4. You will get exposed to your own inefficiencies.
5. Prior experience of having an EA was not good.

There is no doubt that you need to pay additional money to hire an EA but if you compare it with cost of your time, you will be astonished to realize that the cost of EA might be less than 1/10th or 1/20th of the cost which you are incurring because of your time being spent on administrative or unproductive activities.

Similarly, the extra time spent while training the EA is an investment that is going to reward you with exemplary returns.

The next question may come to your mind- what kind of candidate you should hire as an EA? Here is the small checklist:

1. It's better to hire a female candidate for EA profile.
2. EA should be residing within a distance of 30-45 minutes from your office to ensure stability.
3. She must have worked in an EA profile or as a coordinator in immediate previous role.
4. Christians and South Indian females are considered to be more stable and sound on integrity.
5. She should be married and settled in family life.

I learned this habit from my dear friend and India's famous business coach Rahul Jain.

Habit–11 : Meditation

You might be little surprised to notice that I have included Meditation as a time creating habit here. Your reaction is justified because we all look at meditation in the context of spirituality. My experience with meditation is that in addition to peace of mind, it also helps me saving huge amount of time as a by-product.

Let me explain you how.

When I meditate, my awareness improves and reaction reduces. I have observed myself that lot of time goes into making decisions during the day, sometime small ones and sometime big ones. Taking decision means making a choice out of more than one option available. If you also observe closely, lots of mental energy and time gets invested in decision-making. Meditation helps me in taking faster decisions, which in turn speeds up my efficiency and effectiveness.

If you have ever tried meditation, you might be relating to what I am trying to explain here. If you have never done meditation and willing to give it a try, start with a guided meditation. Thanks to this technology era, meditation is easily available and accessible. I would highly recommend trying this App named *Calm*, which I personally use. You may first try with the free version and if you like it, I would recommend to subscribe the paid version to unlock all guided meditations. The best part is that each meditation is just 10-15 minutes long that can easily be done anytime and anywhere.

Habit–12 : Unsubscribe on monthly basis

Time spent on unsubscribing unwanted mails and WhatsApp groups on monthly basis is a great investment in creating time.

You may not think it significant but the casual attention to unwanted mails consumes lot of time. Further, quantity of new mails also overwhelms. I invest 15-30 minutes every month to unsubscribe the mails, which I don't want to receive. It keeps my inbox completely uncluttered.

In case of WhatsApp, you must activate the option *Nobody* under *Who can add me to Groups* in *Privacy settings* so that you can choose to join a group or not.

Habit–13 : Hire a driver

If you self drive to office and it takes more than 45 minutes on one side, you must consider hiring a driver. It will not only save more than 90 minutes per day but will make you hugely efficient. I know people who drive more than 90 minutes on one side every day to their office that means they are wasting more than 3-4 hours on being alert.

I remember that I bought my first car in 2006 and within 5-6 months, I hired a driver when I calculated the time, which I was spending on driving. I had just started my own company in 2005 and financial situation was not conducive to accommodate a driver. Now, when I look back, it was one of the wisest decisions that I took which paid rich dividends in terms of creating huge time and making me super efficient.

The greatest advantage of driver accrues while you are returning back from office. You can take a relaxing nap while your favorite music is playing in the background. Just imagine how fresh you will feel when you reach back home where your family is waiting for you. Moreover, your driver can take lot of your personal chores as well i.e. dropping or picking somebody, sending some stuff to somebody etc.

Most of the people give excuse that they drive because they love driving or they feel in control. However, I fail to understand how can you enjoy driving in a metro city during office hours when the average speed never goes beyond 60, especially when your car is not automatic.

Habit–14 : Unstacking of problems

Have you heard the story of an old woodcutter who was on his deathbed and shared an important life lesson with his five sons?

Let me share it again to drive my point.

The old man was always worried about his five sons quarrelling each other. He tried to make them understand many times but nothing worked. On that fateful day, he asked his eldest son to bring one stack of 4-5 wood sticks. He told them to break this stack. Each one of them tried but could not break the stack of wood sticks. The old man asked them to unstack the wood sticks and now try breaking individual stick. As was expected, it was quite easy for them to break the individual wood stick.

The usual moral of the story is unity is strength.

When we are faced with many problems in life, we become paralyzed from taking action. This state of mind waste huge amount of our productive time. The solution lies in this story- unstack the bundle of problems and break one of it at a time.

Just try this habit and you will be amazed at its workability.

Habit-15 : Avoid reading newspaper

This may sound very difficult if your morning starts with a cup of tea and newspaper. If you observe closely, majority of newspaper put the negative news on the front page because negativity sells. Whatever we read shapes our thoughts.

When you stop reading newspaper, you cultivate two immediate benefits - 1. You save yourself from the negative thoughts at the start of day (which automatically boost your efficiency). 2. You save precious morning time, which can be utilised on what really matters for you i.e., exercise, meditation, helping your spouse etc.

If you can't stop reading newspaper, I would suggest you to shift the timing to afternoon. At any cost, you must protect your morning energy that defines the course of the day and also boost your productivity levels.

Another alternative is to start reading a business newspaper that will enhance your overall knowledge and satisfy your craving for general news as it also carries a page or two on this subject.

Habit–16 : Convert your car into a university on wheels

"I am really fond of reading books but I don't get time to read" OR "There was a time when I used to read but somehow other priorities of life took over". Do you find some association with these types of statements?

These are some of the reasons that people give when I ask about their reading habits.

I can testify that reading books on a consistent basis is not an easy habit to practice. Around 10 years ago I came across a brilliant idea to overcome all the possible excuses related to reading books.

Inspiration came from the book *Who will cry when you die* wherein author *Robin Sharma* outlines how one can utilize commuting time to and from office. The idea was so simple that it struck a chord in my heart immediately. He suggested listening to audio books to use commuting time-that's it!

That was my 'Aha' moment. I loved the suggestion so much that I immediately bought few audio books and started listening while going to and coming back from office. Gradually, it became an effortless habit that I look forward to every morning. Ten years ago, very few books were available in audio format but still there was enough material to listen. These days, all the popular book titles are available in the form of CD's or can be downloaded on your mobile device, online.

While writing about this habit, I suddenly realized that I must have listened to audio books for more than 1,500 hours in the last ten years (around 150 hours per year). If I convert this time into working days of 8 hours, the figure comes to whopping 185 working days. Just this statistic blew me away completely and I feel so good about myself.

This single habit has enriched my life so much that I can't stop talking about it. In addition to infusing positivity and energy into my mornings, it helped me to find answers to a lot of my questions related to different aspects of life.

The best thing about audio books is that often, the book is available in the voice of its author. It helps in understanding the emotional emphasis of the author from the tone at various stages of the book.

If the idea appeals to you, download the App of any service provider and subscribe to the plan, which suits the requirement. My favorite App is Audible. Initially, I opted for the free trial and I was allowed to listen to one audio book free of cost for 30 days. I loved it so much that I took a paid subscription. The best part about Audible is that I can return any audio book within one year of purchase without assigning any reason and can buy another book as a replacement.

If you are not tech savvy, you can buy audio books in CD format through any nearby book store or any e-commerce website.

Happy listening to audio books:)

Habit–17 : Advantage of starting or reaching early

I know, you must have heard about it many times before as well, may be from your teachers or parents or somebody you admire. You might have tried it as well but may not have been able to continue.

However, if you get aware of the amazing advantages of starting early, you might like to give it a solid try. It just doesn't mean getting up early or reaching office early etc. but much more than that. Let me share few advantages which I have personally experienced due to this habit and some of which might be relevant for you as well:

1. The best advantage of starting early for office is that you don't get traffic. In addition to saving time in absolute sense, it also enhances your mental peace when you have a smooth ride to office. However, the best part is your productivity level in office as there is nobody to disturb you. I reach office by 8.15am.

2. You can only keep up with this habit of starting early for office when you also start early back to home in the evening. In this case as well, there are two advantages—one, you save time and second you emotional state remains stable due to insignificant

traffic on the way. I usually come back home by 6 to 6.30pm.

3. If you have a flight to catch at 9am in the morning and distance from your home to airport is 60 mins. and you need to reach airport at least 90 minutes before the flight time, this means you need to leave from your home by 6.30am. I have observed that most of the people usually start from their home around 6.40am. However, I always start 30 minutes before the ideal time, which means 6am in this case. The biggest advantage which I experience is zero anxiety or stress during this one hour time from home to airport and I utilise this time very well. Same thing I experience when I reach airport for check-in and security check. This 30 minutes of starting early gives you an absolute advantage of at least three times (saving) in addition to peace of mind. Isn't it a great return on investment?
4. You can apply the same logic for meetings as well. This will also save time (which otherwise gets wasted in anxiety of getting late) and bless you with peace of mind in addition of increasing your respect in other person's eyes. I usually reach 15-30 minutes before the scheduled meeting time and utilise this time for reading on my Kindle device or do some ideation.
5. I make sure to reach at least 15-30 minutes before the start of any conference, workshop or seminar to meet like-minded people. When you reach early, you find very handful of people which provides excellent opportunity to network with them. Many

times, you get a chance to interact with speakers when you reach before time.

6. If you are learning any skill or sport, try reaching before the scheduled time and you will get almost personal attention and training from the trainer or coach. I tried this when I started learning swimming. The scheduled time was 6am and no student reached before 6.15 or 6.30am. This 15-30 minutes advantage is enough to learn faster and better.
7. If you don't like going to a mall for shopping just because of crowd and the waiting time before trial room, try reaching there at the time when the mall opens in the morning i.e. 11am. There would be two advantage of this strategy - 1. You will find negligible customers that time so you need not wait for trail room. 2. You will find all the sizes and colours at one place as they organize and put back everything before they close for the day. In addition to this, you will save lot of time while making payment as well. This strategy works even on Sundays:)

Habit–18 : KonMari checklist

My friend Rohan Bansal sent me an e-mail few years ago wherein he shared the synopsis of a book named *Life Changing Magic of Tidying Up* by a Japanese author *Marie Kondo*. The content of the e-mail was so engrossing that I couldn't help buying it immediately on my Kindle device. The book actually changed my life forever and how I relate to things which are around me i.e. clothes, shoes, books and a lot more.

You might be wondering how it is related to creation of time. There is a direct relation and that's why I am mentioning about it.

You must have observed that many time you end up buying some stuff because of sudden impulse or poor decision making at the time of purchase, which you actually don't use. The stuff can be clothes, shoes, bedsheets, towels, electric items, etc. It includes low value to high value items. You store this stuff somewhere and forget it or you come across it and regret buying. This creates negative energy and entangles your thought process which consumes unnecessary time, it's so subtle that you don't even notice.

Marie has devised an amazing tidying method which is truly magical. Once you apply the method, your space will be uncluttered forever, yes forever. They way she describes the whole process, it feels like a spiritual experience when you start taking action. You are able to say bye-bye to things that doesn't spark joy with lot of love and respect.

You have to read the book to believe me.

Habit-19 : Buy best in class products

You might be surprised at first by reading the title of this habit. In my life, this habit has saved huge amount of time. We all buy certain important products which have a longer use life i.e. mobile phone, laptop, AC, refrigerator, washing machine, vacuum cleaner etc. When we are taking the buying decision, we tend to avoid the best in class tool because of the price tag and we consider it expensive or not worth the price.

Let me tell you a market secret- no company earns an abnormal profit. You can't judge a product unless you use it over a period of time. It's a thumb rule that expensive products are usually better in quality and performance when you consider the lifetime value.

You might still be thinking--may be if I agree with this but how it is related to saving or creating time? It is related.

You save a lot of time by having either no breakdown or negligible breakdown of the product. Yes, if you consider deeply, it's a huge value addition. Right now, I am writing this chapter on my MacBook Air, which is in its 6th year of use and not even once, I have experienced any issue.

If you recall, you might have already experienced this with reference to certain products at one point of time in your life.

6

CHAPTER

BONUS TOOLS

> **Bad news is that time flies. Good news is that you are the pilot.**

Information technology or IT has become an integral part of our life. Out of which, Internet has become almost indispensable like oxygen. However, IT is just a tool to make our life more efficient and effective with better state of mind. I have been a big fan of technology since beginning and used it to make my life easier and happier. There are some amazing IT tools including Apps which has created huge time for me and I use them on regular basis.

In this bonus chapter, I am sharing these tools and Apps which you can apply immediately to experience the huge quantity of time you save.

1. **LastPass:** Once you install the LastPass App on your device, you need not remember any passwords except just one password. In today's digital world, we

need a user id and a password for almost everything and remembering ID and Password is a painful affair. Beauty of LastPass is that it works across all your devices. It is considered to be the safest password App in the world. It has a free version and paid version. In free version, you can access it on only one device and paid version allows you to access it on any of your devices.

You just need to enter your User IDs and Passwords in the LastPass once and after that whenever you will open that webpage, LastPass will autofill the User ID and Password. You need to key in your LastPass password every time you open the browser because LastPass automatically logs off once you close the browser as a security feature.

I am using the free version of LastPass App on my laptop only as I don't require it on my phone or other devices. I am using it for more than 4 years.

2. **SecureSafe:** SecureSafe is a password vault and it's different from LastPass. In SecureSafe, you can store your important passwords and other details including your debit card grid detail so that you can access it anywhere even if you don't have your debit card with you. It's an App which you can install on your phone.

   I always struggle to remember the PIN of my Credit Card as I don't use it regularly. In such situation SecureSafe comes handy.

   This App claims to offer a level of security comparable to a Swiss bank and it was developed by a Swiss company. I am using it for more than 5 years and more than happy with its performance.

3. **Alfred and Keybreeze:** Alfred is an app and its main function is to access any website through a short cut key. If you access websites on laptop or desktop, then you can't afford not to have this App. For example, I use ICICI Bank website quite frequently, so I don't need to go to the browser and type www.icicibank.com, I just open Alfred App by pressing Command + Spacebar, type ICICI and webpage gets opened where in I just need to key in my User ID and Password. In my case, it gets automatically filled up as I use LastPass.

   The beauty of Alfred is that you can save the address of a particular webpage of a website and when you type the short name assigned to that webpage, it directly gets opened up instead of going through the home page of the website.

   Here is the screen shot for reference:

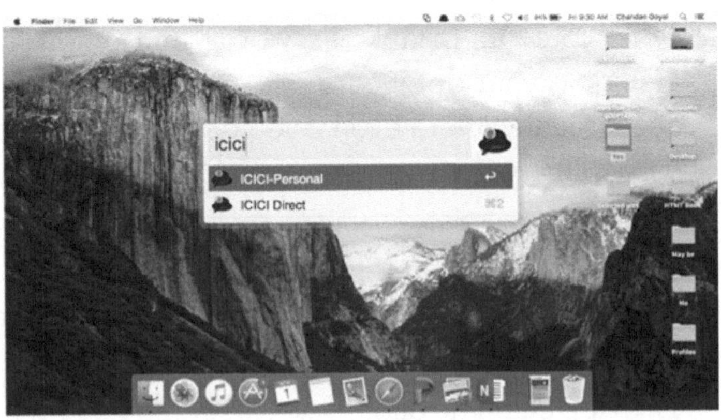

In addition, you can also search any file in your system at lightning speed through Alfred. Even you can search a file based on any keyword it contains inside of file.

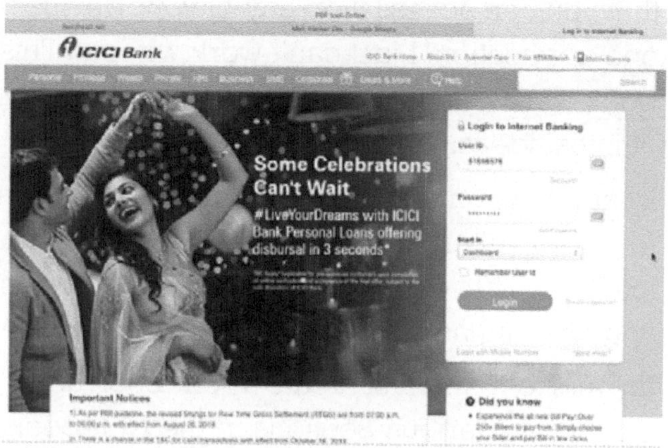

You can even perform random calculations on Alfred:

Alfred App has been specifically designed for Mac iOS so it won't work on Windows.

If you are a Windows user, don't get disheartened as I have a great option for you as well- Keybreeze.

The function and features of Keybreeze are exactly the same, so I am not repeating the same here.

4. **OneNote:** It's a very powerful and useful application to keep all your notes and information at one place in a very organized manner. The beauty of OneNote is that you can access it on any of your devices. This is one application, I just can't work without. This whole book was written in OneNote including jotting down of initial ideas.

   I rate it the most powerful application made by Microsoft after Excel. Its use is very simple and intuitive. The content gets saved automatically as you type. It has a brilliant in-built recorder as well.

   In OneNote, you first create a Notebook and then you can create various Sections in the Notebook. Under each Section you can have as many Page as you want to store your information. It's search feature is simply amazing and it allows to search even the keywords which are in the picture you saved on a Page.

   To use all the amazing features of OneNote, I would recommend to watch few YouTube videos about OneNote. It will help you to get started in much organized fashion and you will be able to use it very optimally.

   If you attend workshop or seminars, you can make all your notes in OneNote. When you ideate upon anything, you can record your insights in OneNote. If you observe a good piece of information in magazine, newspaper or on the web which you might require later on, you can store it in OneNote.

   I can guarantee that you will keep thanking me for it when you will start using it.

5. **Calm:** As the name suggests, Calm is a meditation App. It has contributed huge calmness in my life. A calm mind is the most productive mind as well. There is a free version and paid version of this App, I would suggest you to go for the paid version. You will get the value of money invested in less than one week of using it and after that what you get is simply a bonus.

   Calm has a variety of guided mediations. The beauty is that duration of each meditation is between 10-15 minutes. I use Calm App 2-3 times in a day. The best use is after lunch when I feel little sleepy. After listening a meditation, I feel completely relaxed and energised.

6. **Fiverr:** Fiverr is an online Freelance Services Marketplace wherein you can get some amazing work done at a highly reasonable price with a very fast turnaround time. Some examples of work which you can get done at Fiverr are:

   a. Designing of logo

   b. Designing of visiting card

   c. Animation video

   d. Brochure

   e. Infographics

   f. Voice over

   g. Power point presentations

   h. Website designing

   i. Content writing

j. Translation services

k. SEO services

The basic service package starts at 5$ and that's why it's name is Fiverr. I have used its services for a number of things and it's simply outstanding. If you are not satisfied with the work of seller, you don't pay for it. Freelance service providers around the globe are on Fiverr. Whatever work you can imagine for your business, you will find a freelance service provider who can do that job for you in the fastest turnaround time.

7. **Dunzo:** Dunzo is an App which works as your local delivery and pick up person in your city. Dunzo stands for Done Job! I have become a big fan of Dunzo since they started their service in Noida. You just need to specify the pick up location and delivery location along with description of stuff to be picked up or delivered anywhere in the city.

   I remember: one evening I had craving for Malai Ghevar of Haldiram which is a seasonal sweet. I checked on some food delivery App but only a few packed products of Haldiram were available and obviously Malai Ghevar was not one of them. I thought of trying Dunzo service for this. It was around 7.15pm and I placed the order for Ghevar pick up from the Haldiram outlet at Spice Mall in Noida. To my surprise, me and my wife were enjoying the delicious Ghevar at 8pm. It worked like magic.

   The amazing feature is that when their person reaches the venue i.e. Haldiram outlet, he sends the picture of Ghevar to be bought and once I confirm, he sends a link for payment which can be paid through Paytm or any other wallet. Another great feature of their service is that it is available 24X7.

This App saves huge amount of time for me and it's highly cost effective as well.

8. **Milkbasket:** Milkbasket is another amazing time-saving App. It's business model is very unique. They deliver milk, groceries, fruits and vegetables by very early morning for the order placed a day before. You might say, what's a big deal about it and how it saves time.

   The thing is that you can place the order, amend it, cancel it till 12am (in the night). Further, you need not check out for the order placed because it automatically does that. The only requirement is that you should have money in your Milkbasket wallet before placing the order.

   How it saves time?

   Many times, we remember the household stuff in the night which has finished and will be required next day early morning for breakfast. Usually, at that time all the shops are closed nearby. In such cases, Milkbasket comes very handy as you can place the order till 12AM in the night and it gets delivered next day by 5 or 6AM at your doorstep without disturbing you. When you wake up, you can just open your main door of home and you will find the Milkbasket order hanging around the knob of your door, for sure.

In another case, when you are returning from a holiday or a business trip late night, you suddenly realise that milk and/or some other necessary stuff is not there which you would require first thing in the morning. Milkbasket comes very handy in such situations and provides huge mental peace along with saving time.

9. **Strides:** This is a great habit-building App. Do you know how habits are built? Habits are built through repetition and tracking. Strides help in tracking the habit. There is a very old saying- what gets measured, gets done.

   You can specify the target of any particular habit which you want to develop and track it on regular basis. It works like a game and you start enjoying it. For example, I wanted to develop to read business newspaper on daily basis which I was not doing. I created a habit in Strides that I should read the business newspaper at least 5 times a week and whenever I read the newspaper I ticked that habit for the day. This is a screen shot of my three habits on day one of the week:

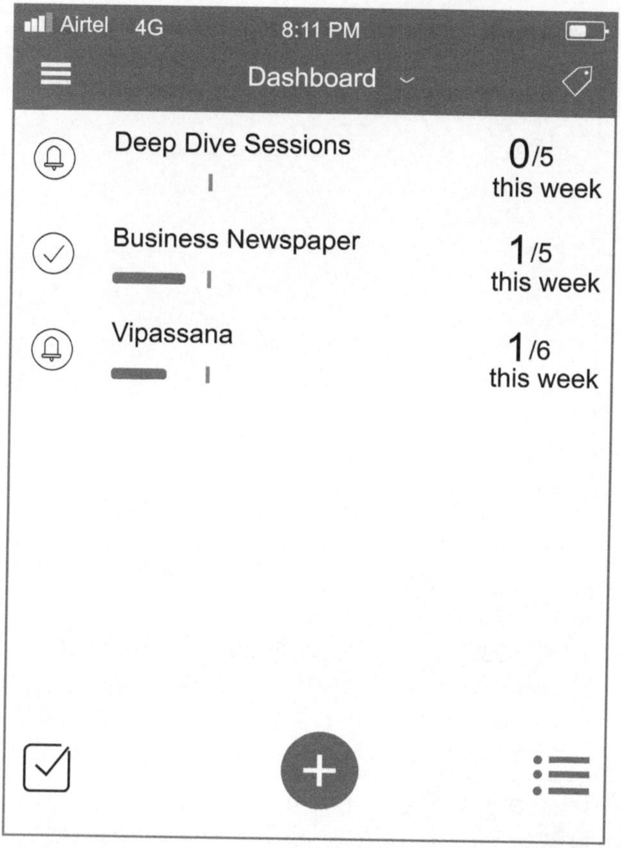

10. **Dictation:** You might be aware about this feature, but I am still sharing at the risk of being repetitive. These days all good smart phones have dictation feature built in. Moreover, the accuracy level has become almost perfect. When you open your keyboard in any application, an icon of microphone also appears on it- this is the dictation tool. Here is the screen shot for your reference:

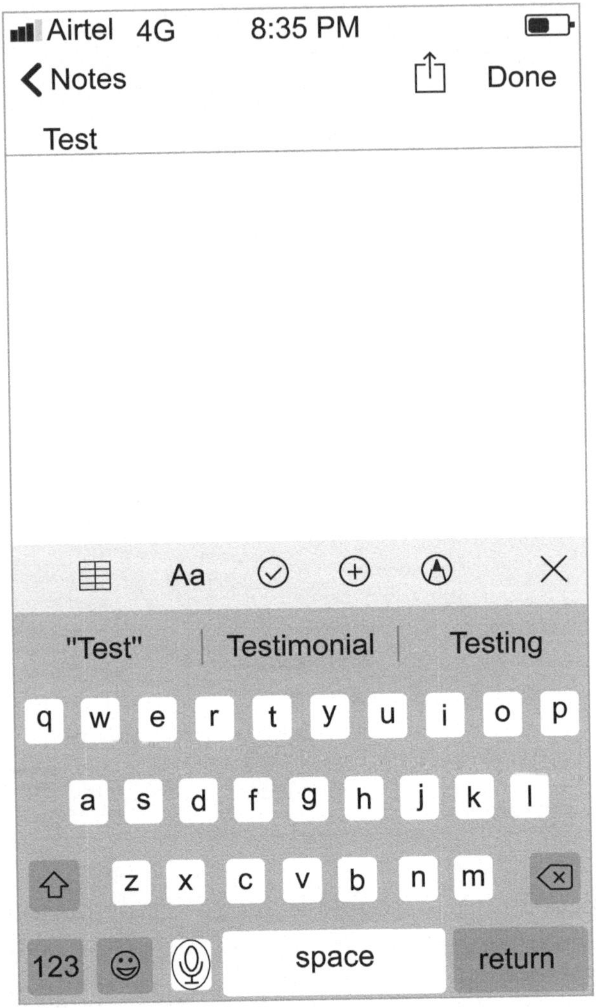

The dictation tool saves huge amount of time by avoiding the requirement of typing, though not completely as you need to format the dictated text a bit. Initially, when you start using the dictation tool, your may get conscious while speaking as you don't get words easily but it gets settled down as you start using it.

11. **Small PDF:** There are many tools to convert a file from Word/Excel/PPT/JPEG format to PDF and vice versa but nothing comes closer to Small PDF when you compare it's speed and simplicity.

    In addition to conversion, you can also do compression, splitting, merging, unlocking of a protected PDF file and protecting a PDF file etc.

    I am using it for more than 5 years and this is the best tool I have come across. You can simply go to www.smallpdf.com and do any task on a file with quite intuitive and self explanatory user interface. They also have a Chrome Extension.

7

CHAPTER

FAQS AND SOLUTIONS

> **Raindrops may be little in shape and size but their continuous fall makes a river overflow. Remember, small consistent efforts make massive changes in life.**

You have almost completed this book and reached to the last chapter. Some of the questions listed here may come across as quite trivial, so you may be tempted to skip them. However, my advice is to go through each of the FAQs listed here to get some more insights.

1. **How to schedule for vacation when I am not sure whether I'll be able to go for vacation when the time arrives?**

   Book the flight ticket and hotel (non-refundable), declare it to people in advance and keep sharing about it after some interval so that it gets in their mind. You'll be amazed how situations in life conspire to make sure that you go on vacation. I have experienced it many times. Few times, it was as close as just one day before the vacation and it seemed that this time I might have to cancel my vacation but something happened and situation favored. Not only I went for vacation, the same turned out to be the most memorable ones.

2. **What to do when I am experiencing squeeze of time in every area of my life?**

   The solution is ideation. Write down all the things in your ideation notebook that are going on in your life seeking your attention and time. Now, look at each one of it and assess whether you can take some help, delegate it or outsource completely. If it needs to be done by you, write down the tentative time to do it.

   Once you go through each item of the list, you will experience a feeling of being in control. Further, few of items will be stroked off either not required now or you'll delegate/outsource the same. Most of the time, it's not the shortage of time but the anxiety because so many things are going on and we develop of fear of missing out something.

3. **How to overcome my anxiety before the start of deep dive session?**

   Firstly, it's not easy to have an undivided attention for 60 minutes on something. The easiest way to get over with the anxiety is to do deep breathing for 1-2 minutes before you start the deep dive session. It actually helps in gathering your focus that further helps you in getting started.

4. **What are some productive things that I can do when I get some spare time i.e. 10-15 minutes?**

   10-15 minutes is a lot of time which can be utilised for the following productive stuff:

   - Guided meditation (i.e., Calm app)
   - Inspiring video (i.e., TED Talk)
   - Deep thinking on any issue
   - Talk to some loved ones without any agenda
   - Read few pages of some book or magazine (not newspaper)
   - Writing down things in your capture tool that are going on in your mind.
   - Go for a walk
   - Read about some topics that you find "interesting". (i.e. US-China Trade war, Br-exit etc.).
   - Go through any report which you are avoiding

5. **Can I do ideation at my home or office?**

   If possible, always do your ideation outside home or office. Coffee shop is the best place. The idea is get away from your usual places i.e. home or office for some fresh thinking. Little voice in your brain will try to convince you to do it at home, get lukewarm result and then it will also tempt you to discontinue. Ideation is very discomforting for mind, as it never wants to come out of its comfort zone.

6. **Is there a way I can start getting up early?**

   Instead of focusing on getting up early, focus on how you can go to bed early. Once, you manage to go to bed on time, getting up won't be a big challenge. You must enjoy an uninterrupted sleep of 7-8 hours to remain fresh whole day. So, if you want to get up at 5AM, you must go to bed latest by 10PM. You can do few things which work as indicator to go to sleep—switch on the yellow lights in the evening around 9pm (white lights send signal to your mind to stay alert or awake), play some soothing music, brush your teeth etc. You can develop some customised indicators on your own through creative thinking.

7. **I am experiencing boredom with scheduling, what to do?**

   It's quite natural to get bored sometime with any habit and it's same with scheduling. Don't attach any other meaning to this situation. Don't you feel bore sometime while brushing your teeth but you never skip it, right?

   Further, major reasons of boredom from scheduling are either not getting result from scheduling or not being able to adhere to the schedule. Don't resist or fight with feeling of boredom, rather accept it gracefully. Once you accept it, this feeling automatically loosens its grip on you.

   In such a situation, it would be good if you review the chapters on Ideation, Scheduling and Deep dive session to get the push. While reviewing, you may also get something that may help you immensely.

8. **How to identify a task that I should delegate or outsource?**

   You should delegate an activity for which you

already have a resource but which may not be well trained. Delegation requires immense patience and handholding. Most of the time, you will have an urge to do an activity yourself because delegating it to someone may require some briefing or training and you may not like the quality of work done. This approach may work for some non-recurring work but for any recurring work (even if it recurs in 3-4 months time), you must delegate. This also helps in growth of your subordinates and they will be thankful to you forever in their life for your trust and training.

For outsourcing any activity or task, the decision will depend on cost benefit analysis of time and money involved. To do the cost benefit analysis, you must be aware of your time cost. For the simplicity, divide your monthly earning by 200 hours and this will give you an indicative hourly rate of your time. For example, if your monthly earning is Rs. 200,000 then your hourly cost of time will be Rs. 1,000 per hour (200,000/200). This would be more relevant while taking outsourcing decision for office related tasks.

It's also important to learn outsourcing of tasks related to your personal life. Thanks to the advent of technology and entrepreneurship in last two decades, you have many options to outsource many mundane tasks. Just Google it and you will find many options around you.

9. I feel guilty of reducing my work hours

This is simply because we all give more weightage to quantity than quality. Why we do that? It's easier to track and measure quantity than quality. So, earlier if you were working for 10-11 hours a day, you will experience a drastic reduction of 1-2 hours per day. The little voice in your head will question this reduction of time and label it as "you are taking your focus away" or "your work will suffer this way".

Since you are also habitual of working so hard, there is a good probability that you will buy this argument. In such a situation, you just need to be aware that it takes some time while your mind accepts a new habit. Your mind hates change even if it's beneficial.

10. Why I end up worrying about what I couldn't complete today out of my schedule?

It's a missing tile syndrome and each one of us suffers from it. It means if there is ceiling that is covered with tiles and out of approx. 100 tiles only one tile is missing, your focus will always be on that missing tile and not on the 99 tiles which are perfectly placed.

Similarly, your mind will always focus on the tasks that you couldn't complete and discount the ones, which you completed including some tasks that you were resisting for months. Train your mind to celebrate the completed tasks on daily basis. You may look at your Calendar and To-Do list at the end of the day and just feel grateful for the tasks, which got completed. Just rewind the completion of these tasks in your mind as a movie. Gratitude and worry can't co-exist.

11. Is there any good App to track my habits?

Habit formation is the easiest way to create as

much time as you want. Most of the habits don't go beyond few days once the initial euphoria dies down. To maintain the momentum, tracking of habits plays a significant role. Further, if the habit tracking involves a community, chances of success becomes brighter as we don't want to look bad before our community members and we somehow pull it along till it becomes effortless.

Nike running App is great example of habit tracking within a community environment.

For individual habit tracking, I have tried a number of Apps that are available on iOS but Strides is the best one which I am using for almost 2 years. Its interface is quite easy and you can set up within minutes. The best part is it's animated celebration once I complete all of my habits for the day.

A word of caution: Never set more than 3 new habits for tracking. Moreover, start with some very easy habits, master them and then move on to some tough ones. Minimum time period to track any habit is 3 months before it becomes automatic.

12. How to overcome my distraction of phone?

Let me share few hacks to make your phone an ally rather than your boss. I am talking about these features or setting in the context of iPhone. If you are using any other platform like Android, please find out the similar type of feature or setting in your phone.

Switch off all the notifications including banner notifications that you get to see *on the locked screen* of the phone. I know, little voice in your head will say-no way I can't do this with certain Apps. Believe me, I would even suggest you to switch off notifications even for Apps like Uber, Paytm, etc. Try it for few days and you will understand what I am talking about.

Most of the users switch off the notifications but their missed call and messages still gets displayed on the locked screen of their phone. So, when they look at their phone just to check the time in the locked mode, they get to see those missed call and messages which tempt them to open the phone and then they are gone for a good 15-20 minutes with no value addition in the middle of an important work.

(a) Always read any article on Safari in reading mode wherein you don't get to see any ads or clutter of the web page. Moreover, the font size also gets bigger which helps you to concentrate and read faster. To make reading mode as default, just long press those four lines on the top left of your Safari browser and select the option Use on All Websites.

(b) Add the screen time widget to monitor where and how much time you are spending on your phone. In case you are not aware about this feature, just Google it and try to find it.

(c) Don't keep more than 8-10 Apps on one screen. These are in addition to four Apps at the bottom that remains the same on all the screens. Don't keep more than 3 screens and the third screen should only contain folders, which keep all your Apps that you don't require on regular basis.

(d) Switch on Night Shift mode at least 4 hours before you go to sleep. It changes the color of your screen from blue to yellow that reminds you to slow down and get away from your phone.

13. Why I experience so much resistance to fill up my self-created time sheet?

Simply because you don't want to face the truth which reveals your time wasting and unproductive patterns. Moreover, it also creates a feeling of being accountable to somebody. Given a choice, we don't want to be accountable for anything in life but we do because of certain compulsions.

Once you understand and digest this, it becomes a lot easier to beat the resistance of time sheet. If you want to fill it up joyfully, create a strong purpose i.e. increase in productivity, to identify tasks which you can delegate or outsource, track your effort on a specific project which is time bound. In fact, you can also keep a count of deep dive sessions in your time sheet.

There is a fair chance that you may not be able to recall the time spent even a day earlier if you skip and it might frustrate you, prompting you not to fill it up or defer it by one more day. To ensure that you fill up time sheet on daily basis, set up a daily recurring reminder in your phone. Treat yourself on weekly basis for filling up time sheet consistently. The reward, however small it may be, will motivate you to achieve your targets.

CONCLUSION

That you have reached to this chapter is a testimony that you are really interested to learn and master the art of creating time. As per my experience, when you read any actionable book, you tend to skip at least 50% points that can be implemented right away in your life. Why? For the simple reason that we all think that let me first finish the book and then I'll apply the actionable steps in my life.

Well, though there is no problem with this thinking but there is a strong possibility that you might forget some of the actionable items or you just might like to relax as you have done a big task of finishing a book, isn't it?

Actual result of any insight or knowledge lies in its implementation; otherwise it just gets reduced to another piece of information. A study has revealed that real benefit from self-help comes in the second reading. I have also experienced it. If I like a self-help book, I always make sure to read it twice. To my surprise, lot of content seemed new in the second reading which might have skipped registering in mind. So, I would sincerely invite you to give this book a second reading.

However, just for the ease of your reference, I am listing down key concepts and actionable points:

1. You should not manage time rather you should manage "distractions". If there is no distraction, time can be managed with ease and grace.
2. Absence of clarity or purpose for the free time always lead to another distraction.
3. Ideation and scheduling is antidote to distraction.
4. Spending time with oneself is the biggest source of creating time.
5. Ideation without execution is an illusion.
6. Trinity of scheduling:
    a. Capture tool
    b. Calendar
    c. To-do list
7. What should be scheduled first? Remember the story of Professor and glass jar.
8. If you don't have a well-maintained schedule, then you are attending stuff or doing things as per somebody else's schedule or priorities.
9. Deep dive session is the Brahmastra [the ultimate tool] of all the time creation tools.
10. Deep dive session will put you in a league where these is no competition.
11. Check e-mails only TWICE a day.
12. Learn to say 'NO'.
13. Simplify, Simplify & Simplify.

14. Hotel checks in for ideation and deep dive sessions.
15. Pooch daala to life jhingalala!
16. Declare an odd completion time before call or meeting.
17. Unsubscribe on monthly basis.
18. Convert your car into a university on wheels.
19. Follow KonMari checklist.